BOOK OF HOUSEHOLD HINTS

Edited by Mary Crockett

W & H Publications

W & H Publications, a division of W & H Specialist
Publications Limited
P O Box 90119, Auckland Mail Centre, Auckland, New Zealand
Phone: (64 9) 360 3820 Fax: (64 9) 360 3831
Email: whpubs@listener.co.nz
Website URL: http://www.wilsonandhorton.co.nz

This book is copyright. Except for the purposes of fair reviewing, no part of this publication may be reproduced or transmitted in any form or by any means, electronic or mechanical, including photocopying, recording, or any information storage and retrieval system, without written permission from the publisher. Infringers of copyright render themselves liable to prosecution.

Editing: Mary Crockett
Design: Derek Watts

© 1999 New Zealand Woman's Weekly and W & H Publications

ISBN 1 -877214-04-3

Printed by Hutcheson, Bowman & Stewart, Wellington

The hints in this book are the New Zealand Woman's Weekly readers' own suggestions and not those of the editor or publisher. While every care has been taken in the compiling and printing of these hints, the publisher takes no responsibility for the effect or results of using the hints and cannot accept responsibility for any errors, inadvertent or not, that may be found or may occur at some time in the future for any reason.

Contents

Chapter One	OUT, DAMNED SPOT! / Stain removal	7
Chapter Two	AT THE HEART OF IT / Kitchen capers	...............**16**
Chapter Three	ALL STEAMED UP / Bathroom basics	..................**28**
Chapter Four	SOAP SUDS AND GLORY / Laundry lore	...............**34**
Chapter Five	ELBOW GREASE AND VINEGAR / Cleaning up	......**44**
Chapter Six	POTTING AND PAINT / Gardening and DIY	........**54**
Chapter Seven	MAKING A MEAL OF IT / Food tricks	.....................**66**
Chapter Eight	ANYTHING AND EVERYTHING / General hints	....**94**
Index		....................**113**

Acknowledgements

Grateful thanks to the readers of the New Zealand Woman's Weekly who have made this book possible. We are indebted to Tui Flower, for many years director of the New Zealand Woman's Weekly Test Kitchen, whose knowledge and experience of cooking and home economics was of much assistance in checking the manuscript. We also acknowledge with thanks the advice from Bhaidas Bhula of the New North Pharmacy and Charles Nairn of the Unichem Thompson Mace Pharmacy in the sections relating to compounds available from pharmacies.

We gratefully acknowledge permission from Rawleigh's International to use the tin containing their celebrated Antiseptic Healing SALVE as the basis for the cover design. General advice from Rawleigh International Marketing Manager Bev Rawleigh was also welcome.

Trade names have been used in this publication where a description of the compound may have been confusing or unfamiliar. This is not intended as an endorsement of the products mentioned. Other similar substances could be substituted.

Answers to the questions on the back cover:
For a red wine spill on carpet, immediately pour cold water or soda water on and very thoroughly pat dry.
Candles which have been kept in the freezer burn more slowly and evenly.
Boil rhubarb in saucepan for a shine, or to clean burn marks.
Keep your old telephone directory in the car as a reference book for addresses.
Rub mildew marks with baking soda or a mild bleach solution, then rinse in clean water.
Catch slugs in a glass of beer set in the garden, or sprinkle bran around plants.

Introduction

For more than 60 years faithful readers of the New Zealand Woman's Weekly have shared household hints with each other through the pages of the magazine. Now their many and varied suggestions have been collected together for all to share.

In the early days, sophisticated household cleaners were not available. Homemakers relied on kitchen staples for many household cleaning tasks. There were three guiding principles: problems had to be tackled quickly, efficiently and, above all, economically.

Today's supermarket shelves are crowded with an array of commercial cleaning agents and many of us believe the only way to cope with a stain is to reach for the first spray or wipe-on solvent to hand. While many of these products are invaluable, they are not the only answer, and are often more expensive than the remedies our mothers and grandmothers once took for granted.

Modern commercial products frequently have as their base the same chemical ingredients found in home remedies such as cream of tartar, baking soda or vinegar. They may seem to have an extra magic about them. However, the continuing successful use of kitchen staples is demonstrated regularly, in the Woman's Weekly's ever-popular 'Handy Hints' column.

Readers have shared a host of other ingenious ideas over the years*. Cooking, gardening, cleaning and do-it-yourself tips have been offered for many common (and some not-so-common) household dilemmas. The emphasis has always been on making life easier.

This collection is a fascinating and imaginative guide to running a contemporary home. It shows that practical and money-saving ideas never date.

* Where several alternative solutions are offered to a particular problem, these are indicated in the text with bullet points.

CHAPTER ONE

Out, Damned Spot!

STAIN REMOVAL

ADVISORY NOTE
- Treat stains promptly.
- Use a simple treatment first then repeat, as many stains lessen gradually.
- Sponging with cool water is often the safest treatment. Hot water and soap can set stains.
- Test all stain removal chemicals in a hidden part of the article – inside seams or hems, or under collar.
- Thorough rinsing out of all treatment is important.
- Treat stain from the underneath side of the fabric where possible. Hold an old piece of towel underneath to absorb stain as it is treated.
- Avoid rubbing hard on stained area. Dab the stain, working into the centre of the stain from the outside to prevent spreading.
- Wear gloves when handling strong chemicals.
- Work in well-ventilated area when using solvents. Never use near flames. Read container instructions carefully when using unfamiliar cleaners and chemicals.
- Be aware of treatment, should accidental spills occur.
- Keep all chemicals out of reach of children.
- Always take note of the care labels on garments and check which treatments should not be used on the material.

Clothing

BALLPOINT INK
Dab with methylated spirits, allow to dry, then wash normally.

BERRY AND RED FRUIT STAINS ON WHITE COTTON
- Immediately soak in tepid water, then wash normally. Repeat if necessary.
- If stains are old, stretch stained area over a bowl, and pour hot water through it.
- Sponge with peroxide solution, then rinse.
- On washable materials other than cotton, soak stained area in glycerine for about an hour, then wash in detergent, using warm water, and rinse.
- For other stubborn fruit stains, cover stain with borax and run hot water through it.

BLOOD STAINS
- Soak at once in tepid water, then wash normally.
- Soak in lightly salted tepid water.

CHEWING GUM
- Rub the spot well with a piece of ice in a plastic bag to harden the gum. Scrape off as much as possible, then dab the remaining stain with methylated spirits. Wash in the usual way.
- Tar can be treated in the same way.

CHOCOLATE STAINS
- Sponge in cold water, soak in enzyme powder solution, wash normally and treat any remaining grease mark with solvent.
- Spray on household cleaner such as Spray 'n' Wipe and rinse off with cold water.

COFFEE
- On a pure silk scarf, sponge with lukewarm water, then apply

> **EUCALYPTUS OIL**
> Keep a bottle of eucalyptus oil in the laundry. It removes many stains, including grease, chewing gum and tar. Apply to spot and rub material between the hands. Always follow up with an application of white methylated spirits to get rid of the oily stain left on the fabric. Rub well into the fabric, then wash in the usual way.

glycerine, rubbing very gently between hands. Leave for half an hour, then wash in warm soapy water and rinse well.
- Wash in a solution of enzyme powder and lukewarm water. Do not rub the silk too hard but gently "dunk" up and down. Hard rubbing will disturb the weave of the fabric.
- On other materials, blot up with paper towel, rinse in cold water. Rub in detergent and wash normally

FISH SLIME (INCLUDING SHELLFISH SLIME)
Sponge clothes with a solution of plain salt and warm water to "thin" slime, enabling it to be washed out more easily.

FRUIT STAINS ON WHITE WOOLLENS
Soak for 10-15 minutes in a litre of lukewarm, soapy water to which a tablespoon of hydrogen peroxide has been added. Rinse in lukewarm water before drying.

GREASE SPOTS ON SUEDE SHOES
Rub spots with a clean rag dipped in glycerine.

GREASY COLLARS AND CUFFS
Rub gently with a little ammonia mixed with salt.

GRASS STAINS ON WHITE COTTON
- Soak in cold water overnight then wash as usual.
- Rub with Swarfega, then wash as usual.

- Rub with a cloth dipped in methylated spirits, keeping a cloth pad under the stain.
- Soak in kerosene for several hours then wash in warm, soapy water.

INK STAINS ON LINEN
Cover stain with mustard powder mixed with water, leave overnight then rinse in warm, soapy, water.

INK STAINS ON WHITE BLOUSES AND SHIRTS
Cover marks with thick paste of baking soda and hydrogen peroxide, leave overnight then wash well.

LIPSTICK MARKS
- Wash normally after rubbing area with soap.
- Sponge with white methylated spirits, then wash normally.
- Rub with glycerine, then wash.
- Rub with margarine or lard, then wash immediately.
- For garments that cannot be washed, press a piece of fresh, white bread into the stains.

MUD STAINS
Leave mud until dry, brush with a stiff brush, then sponge with a weak solution of cold water, detergent and ammonia or detergent and baking soda.

NAIL VARNISH ON RAYON AND OTHER SYNTHETIC GARMENTS
- Soak garment in tepid water for an hour, and varnish will peel off.
- Use this method on all smooth-surfaced garments made from synthetic fibres which might dissolve if cleaned with nail-polish remover.

WHITE CORRECTION FLUID STAINS
Rub gently with eucalyptus oil on a clean cloth, then apply white methylated spirits to get rid of the oily stain left on the fabric. Wash normally.

OIL SPOTS ON IMITATION SUEDE
- Place white blotting paper or kitchen paper towel over oil spot and run a warm iron over, to absorb grease.
- Use a spray-on cleaner formulated for oil-based stains. Follow instructions.

OLIVE OIL STAINS
- Spray with aerosol drycleaner. Follow directions on the can, brush cleaner powder off and reapply for stubborn stains. Works well on clothes and upholstery.
- Rub glycerine into stains and leave on overnight. Rub between the fingers next day, then wash with an enzyme powder. Repeat if necessary.

PAINT STAINS
- Rub stained material with a mixture of turpentine and milk. Also lessens dye stains.
- Treat with equal parts of mineral turpentine and cloudy ammonia.
- Treat water-based paint stains while still wet, rinsing in warm water. Wash normally.

PERSPIRATION STAINS
Add two aspirin tablets to the washing water to remove underarm perspiration stains and odours.

YELLOW FRUIT JUICE OR CREAM STAINS ON GREY SWEATSHIRT
Rub glycerine into the stains with fingers. Leave for 20 minutes then rub well with a bar of soap or rub in a paste of soap powder. Wash in washing machine. If necessary, soak in Napisan overnight.

RUST ON A WHITE SHIRT COLLAR
- Wash in soft warm suds, then rinse. Rub plenty of dry washing soda on stain. Leave 12 hours or so rolled up. Then wash in warm suds again.
- Hand-cleaner jellies rubbed in will remove relatively fresh stains and lighten older ones. Apply more as it works in, then

rinse well and wash as usual.
- Moisten stain, rub shaving soap stick gently in on both sides, then rinse well. Repeat, should stain remain.

SCORCH MARKS
- For stubborn marks, apply glycerine, leave for about half an hour then rub with a cloth dipped in a solution of warm water and mild detergent.
- On jersey material, cover stain with a mixture of borax and glycerine. Leave for an hour. Wash as usual.
- On very light scorch marks, press the sticky side of Sellotape over the area. Do not rub.

STICKY LABELS ON COTTON-POLYESTER
- Soak material in glycerine for some hours, allow to dry on and then wash in lukewarm suds.
- Dab on nail polish remover until well soaked, leave for a while and then wash. (Do not use on cellulose acetate garments.)
- Sponge with pure methylated spirits.

YELLOW MARKS ON WHITE SILK
Spread paste of cream of tartar and water over stain. Leave for one hour. Wash in usual way.

Furniture, Floors and Furnishings

CRAYON MARKS ON A BLACKBOARD
- An old nylon stocking will remove the crayon very easily, without damaging the blackboard surface.
- Sponge crayon marks with eucalyptus.
- Damaged surface can be repainted with blackboard paint, available from hardware stores.

CRAYON ON LINOLEUM
Rub with silver polish and finish with a clean cloth.

> **Here's a Hint...**
>
> ## RUG STAINS
> - Failure to get all the moisture out is the cause of almost all rug stains. Regardless of the stain, the main thing is to soak up as much liquid as possible immediately. Use a towel or paper towels. The trick is to blot and blot until all the moisture is out. When patch is almost dry, stand on towel, repeating until no more moisture shows.
> - Next, use a mild solution of vinegar and water to blot any excess stain and then go over it again with clear water. If there is any slight discolouration, go over it again with a mild solution of liquid dishwashing detergent and water. After each treatment, blot up all moisture to avoid staining from carpet backing.
> - Baking soda or cornflour can be sprinkled on as a freshener; these also help to dry up any remaining moisture.

CRAYON ON VINYL WALLPAPER
Rub gently with a cottonwool bud dampened with methylated spirits.

CURRY STAINS ON WHITE TABLE LINEN
- Treat fresh stains immediately by soaking in tepid water. Wash normally. Repeat if necessary.
- Soak old stains overnight in water with borax or cloudy ammonia. Rinse, then soak overnight in Napisan. Wash normally.

FELT PEN AND INK ON PLASTIC
- Rub mark with methylated spirits.

FINGERMARKS ON WALLS
- Rub with a clean pencil eraser.
- Rub with a slice of soft white bread squashed into a ball.

FRUIT STAINS ON TABLE LINEN
Apply a little camphor to stained area before washing.

GREASE SPOTS ON CARPET

Sprinkle baking soda thickly over marks, brush lightly through the pile and leave overnight. Vacuum up, or press with a cool iron over brown paper.

GREASY MARKS ON UPHOLSTERED CHAIR BACKS

- Press powdered chalk or talcum powder lightly into the stain and leave for an hour, then brush or vacuum off.
- Cover marks with chalk or talcum powder, place a dry cloth over and press very lightly with a warm iron. Move the cloth as it becomes soiled. The heat from the iron allows the grease to be absorbed easily. Don't press too hard; go lightly.

HEAT MARKS ON POLISHED WOOD

- Rub the mark gently in a circular motion with brass polish, using a clean, soft cloth. Continue for several minutes. Finish with a protective wood and leather polish.
- Mix cigarette ash, olive oil and linseed oil, spread this over the mark and leave overnight. Next day, rub off and polish well.
- Apply a mixture of olive oil and salt. Leave for half an hour then rub with a soft cloth.
- Put two or three crushed walnuts into a piece of fine cloth, dip into olive oil and gently rub in a circular motion until the mark is cleared. Repeat three or four times.
- Cut a walnut in half and gently rub cut side on mark.
- Rub gently with a little methylated spirits on a soft cloth.

RED WINE SPILLS ON CARPET

Immediately pour cold water or soda water over, soaking area thoroughly. Dry carpet completely with several towels or wads of kitchen towelling. Stand on towels if necessary, to add extra weight and aid absorption.

RED WINE SPILLS ON TABLE LINEN

Immediately put soda water or cold water on stain., then proceed as for berry and red fruit stains.

INK MARKS ON LEATHER
Rub with baking soda and dust off as ink is absorbed. Repeat until mark disappears. If coloured leather, test on an inconspicuous area first.

LAMINATED BENCH OR TABLETOP STAINS
- Rub with some toothpaste on a soft damp cloth.
- Wipe over with damp sponge dipped in powdered bathcleaner. Rinse, then wipe with a cloth sprinkled with kerosene. (Editor's note: Contact the manufacturers for their advice, especially if surface is new.)

RUST STAINS ON METAL
- Rub with raw onion.
- Rub with a cork dipped in olive oil.

WATER STAINS ON GLASS VASES
Fill with a strong solution of malt vinegar and water, leave overnight, then scrub hard with a scouring pad. Rinse well.

WATER STAINS ON AN INNER-SPRUNG MATTRESS
- Sponge with warm water, sprinkle with cornflour, brush thoroughly when dry.
- Buy suitable material and make another cover for mattress. Hand tack on, or tie on with tapes.

YELLOWISH VINYL ON A BEDHEAD
- Wipe with damp sponge and powdered bath cleaner, then with clean, damp sponge.
- Rub with toothpaste on a warm, damp cloth.
- Use an ammonia-based cleanser that is not abrasive.

CHAPTER TWO

AT THE HEART OF IT

KITCHEN CAPERS

Pots and pans, cleaning

BURNT-ON FOOD
- Soak burnt pans and dishes in hot water containing some dishwasher granules. Leave for a couple of hours.
- Add lukewarm water (not hot) and a few spoonfuls of baking soda and let stand overnight.
- Put enough vinegar into bottom of pan to cover base and bring gently to the boil. Cover and leave to cool for half an hour. Clean normally.

BLACKENED PATTY TINS
- Wash discoloured cake tins, patty tins and trays with soda water and steel wool.
- Wash tins in hot soapy water, and rinse well in clean water. (Make sure no grease is left on after washing or it will bake on the next time it is used and be very difficult to clean.)

RUSTY CAKE TINS clean up well if rubbed with a raw potato. Rinse in hot water.

IRON FRYING PAN
- To season, heat a little oil in the pan until hot. Leave to go cold. Wipe out. Repeat if wished.
- To clean, rub with salt and paper and wipe with a damp cloth. Dry thoroughly.

RINSE A FRYPAN in clear water after washing. Prevents tiny particles of grease from clinging and discolouring it when heated.

RUB AN OMELETTE PAN with kitchen towel after use; never wash it.

CLEANING COPPER BASED SAUCEPANS
- Rub pan with salt and lemon juice or a lemon slice.
- Rub with half a tomato, dipped in salt.
- Rub with salt and vinegar.

KEEP ALUMINIUM SAUCEPANS CLEAN when boiling eggs by adding a teaspoon of vinegar to the water.

SHINE UP SAUCEPANS by cooking rhubarb in them.

SPLUTTERING SAUCEPAN LIDS. Push a toothpick under saucepan lid to allow steam to escape when cooking with lid on.

POT LID STORAGE. Store on inside of under-sink cupboard door. Cut a length of curtain wire to suit width of cupboard and attach, using curtain eyes and hooks. Store lids behind wire.

Stovetops

FADING FIGURES ON OVEN SWITCHES can be touched up with a waterproof marker pen.

MATCH THE SIZE OF POTS to the size of stovetop elements for maximum heat efficiency.

MELTED CLINGFILM on stovetops wipes away with nail polish remover. Rinse well with cold water.

SPILLOVERS ON A STOVE TOP. Tackle immediately by softening

with a damp cloth. Carefully scrape lumps away with a knife, then rub with all-purpose cleaner.

REMOVE FATTY OR GREASY STAINS by rubbing gently with steel soap pads or metal-polish.

The Sink

BLOCKED SINK
- Pour down three tablespoons of baking soda and ½ cup of vinegar. Replace plug. After half an hour pour down a jug of boiling water.
- Remove top third of an old tennis ball by cutting with a sharp knife. Place remaining tennis ball piece over plughole, apply the heel of the hand to the top and push sharply. Acts like a plunger.

SINK CLEANING IDEAS
- Fill sink with cold water and add lemons, cut in half. Leave overnight. Next morning, let water run away, rub round sink with lemon halves, then rinse.
- Clean stainless steel sinks with a paste made from baking soda and water.
- Rub hard with dampened newspaper.
- Clean stainless steel sink surrounds with a little vinegar on a damp cloth. Rinse, then dry.

KEEP STEEL SCOURING PADS RUST-FREE by submerging in a jar of water to which a dash of detergent, or teaspoon of baking soda, has been added. Prevents rusting.

PUT A CUP HOOK NEAR THE SINK to hold rings and watches while washing up.

WASTE DISPOSAL ODOURS. Eliminate odours by grinding cut-up orange, lemon or grapefruit rinds while flushing the unit with hot water.

Ovens

OVEN CLEANING WITHOUT SPRAYS
- Paint cleaning gel on top, sides and bottom of stove (after removing elements and trays), leave overnight and wash off next day with soap and water.
- Combine 2 teaspoons baking soda, 1 tablespoon vinegar and 1 cup water, boil for a few minutes, cool slightly, then paint all over oven, trays and racks. Wipe any excess moisture from floor of oven. Heat to 180 degreesC for a few minutes. Cool slightly, and wipe clean.
- Leave a saucer of ammonia in the oven overnight. The ammonia fumes loosen all dirt and grease.

CLEANING SMELLS IN AN OVEN. Heat orange peel inside oven after cleaning to remove odours.

GLASS OVEN DOOR. Clean with a damp cloth dipped in baking soda. When dry, rub with a soft cloth.

MICROWAVE EFFICIENCY. Wipe metal and plastic parts regularly with a damp cloth to avoid build-up around door seals.

MICROWAVE FRESHNESS. Clean with a damp cloth, then place either a sprig of parsley or mint in oven. Turn on for 20 seconds.

The Benchtop

NON-SLIP CHOPPING BOARD. Place a large rubber band over

each end of a wooden chopping board to keep it anchored on a damp benchtop.

CHOPPING BOARD OVER SINK. Buy a chopping board big enough to wedge across sink for extra bench space when sink is not in use.

GREASY, FATTY SPILLS ON THE BENCHTOP come away if sprinkled with a little salt before wiping.

SCRATCHED FORMICA BENCHTOP
- Rub well with a small amount of brass polish.
- Rub with petroleum jelly.
- Rub scratches with a crayon (as near to the colour as possible), then rub over with a cloth dipped in olive oil. Polish as usual.

STAND HOT SAUCEPANS OR FRYING PANS on cork or wood mats to avoid damaging a benchtop.

Washing-up tips

BURNT MARKS ON PLATES can be removed by rubbing them with a cork dipped in damp salt. Cigarette stains can be removed the same way.

CLEAN A METAL CHEESE GRATER with a toothbrush.

SOAK CUTLERY in a jug of water while it is waiting to be washed.

DISCOLOURED CUPS
- Rub with one or two used teabags dipped in a teaspoon of sugar.
- Rub with a dampened cork dipped in salt.
- Rub gently with a small amount of toothpaste, then rinse.

DISHWASHER ODOURS. Sprinkle a little baking soda over the

> **Here's a Hint...**
>
> **USES FOR A TEABAG**
> After brewing, use teabag to:
>
> - Clean spectacles.
> - Clean the splash marks off the window above the sink.
> - Fertilise around roses.
> - Clean cutlery, dishes and frying pan of all grease and food before washing.
> - Prevent bad sunburn (keep dabbing skin with tea and a tea-bag).
> - Clean film smears off car windows.

bottom of tray when dirty dishes are stacked and waiting for a full load.

CLEAN EGG BEATERS under cold tap immediately after use. Never use hot water as it cooks the egg on to the beater.

STAINED TEASPOONS. Rub with baking soda on a damp cloth.

WHEN WASHING DELICATE GLASSES slide them sideways into hot washing-up water to prevent them cracking.

The Fridge and Freezer

CLEAN OUTSIDE OF FRIDGE by spraying with a mixture of ammonia and cold water.

DEFROST A FREEZER twice a year to ensure it works efficiently.

RUBBER SEALS ON THE FRIDGE will last longer if wiped regularly with methylated spirits.

DEFROST A FRIDGE QUICKLY with a small hair drier, but be sure to be careful that drier does not come into contact with any water or damp surfaces.

FRIDGE ODOURS
- Leave a saucer of baking soda, or an open packet of soda, on fridge shelf.
- Sprigs of fresh mint keep fridge fresh.
- Wipe with a paper towel sprinkled with vanilla essence.
- Place a small piece of charcoal in fridge door to absorb fish smells.

MEAL LEFTOVERS PLACED IN EMPTY COFFEE JARS take up less storage space in the fridge. (Any tall thin container is better than a wide-mouthed bowl.)

MILDEW IN THE FRIDGE. Wipe with white vinegar. To prevent mildew building up, wipe fridge seals with vinegar once a month.

PADDED OVEN MITTS protect fingers from the cold when defrosting the deep freeze or searching for food at the bottom of the freezer.

PARTY ICE lasts well if placed in a plastic colander over a large bowl or saucepan. The surplus water can drain away, slowing down the melting rate of the ice.

FREEZING SOUPS AND STEWS. If short of containers, place a plastic freezer bag inside a container and pour in food to be frozen. Later, remove bag and reuse container.

REUSABLE LABELS FOR THE FREEZER. Write on plastic with a washable whiteboard marker.

VACUUM THE COILS at the back of fridge regularly to prevent dust build-up.

Utensils

CAN OPENERS work best if dipped in hot water before use (manual openers only).

EGGSHELL FUNNEL. Half an eggshell with a hole pierced at one end makes a good alternative to a funnel for runny liquids.

FOIL FUNNEL. To pour ingredients into a narrow-necked jar, shape a double layer of aluminium foil into a cone, then snip off the point.

FURRED KETTLE ELEMENT
- Add a tablespoon of citric acid to boiling water in kettle, leave a few minutes, then rinse.
- Boil equal parts vinegar and water, leave in kettle overnight.

NEVER OVERFILL A KETTLE. Make sure the element is covered, but don't heat up more water than is needed.

NEW WOODEN UTENSILS. Soak wooden spoons, chopping boards, etc overnight in cider vinegar before use. Seals the wood and prevents onion or garlic odour being absorbed.

NON-SLIP SPOON HANDLE. Wind a rubber band around spoon handle to prevent spoon from slipping into cake or batter mixture in a mixing bowl.

A POWDER PUFF is useful for dusting flour on pastry boards.

RUBBER SPATULA HEADS. When these become loose, put them on the other end of the handle and they will fit tightly again.

TO OPEN BOTTLE AND JAR LIDS
- Grip top with a sheet of sandpaper, rough side downwards.

- Grip with a length of rubber inner tube.
- Dip in very hot water for a couple of minutes.

VEGETABLE PEELERS. Buy a bright blue peeler – it's less likely to get thrown out with the peelings.

Recycling

BENCHTOP RECYCLING. Save egg shells, banana skins and peelings in an ice-cream container (with lid) on bench. Dig in under bushes in garden instead of compost.

EMPTY PLASTIC MILK BOTTLES ARE USEFUL AS:
- Containers for dry ingredients such as rice or flour. (Dry thoroughly first and fill with a funnel.)
- Kitchen scoops. Screw the top on tightly and cut the body at a gentle angle with a sharp knife. The neck of the bottle becomes the handle.

FLATTEN EMPTY PLASTIC BOTTLES for recycling by first pouring very hot water in until plastic is soft enough to crush.

REFILL PACKS. When decanting coffee and salt from refill packs, cut off two top corners to allow air in and aid flow.

General tips

BURN MARKS ON AN ALUMINIUM SAUCEPAN
- Boil up some rhubarb or apple peelings in pan.
- Cover bottom of pot well with common salt. Pour boiling water over, leave till water is cold. A pot-mit should remove marks easily.

- Bring a little vinegar to the boil in pot, leave to cool with lid on for half an hour, then wash in usual way.
- Boil one or two onions cut in two or three pieces, skin and all, in half pot of water for half an hour and stand aside until next day. Wash as usual.
- Put some ashes and a handful of washing soda in the pot, half fill with cold water, leave to boil for a while with the cover on. Leave until cold, when burn marks should scrape off easily.
- Leave pot in the freezer overnight. Wash in the normal way.
- Boil a solution of two tablespoons cream of tartar with one litre of water, leave to cool then clean with a soap-impregnated pad.

COOKING SMELLS. Fill an uncovered saucepan with hot water, add 1 teaspoon ground cinnamon or ground cloves and boil for about 15 minutes.

DRAIN VEGETABLE PEELINGS in a flower pot by the sink before throwing them out, to get rid of excess moisture.

GRUBBY DISHCLOTHS. Soak in bleach and water overnight. Rinse out.

KEEP FRESH HERBS ON THE WINDOWSILL and flies will stay away. Mint, parsley and basil are particularly effective.

LINE SHELVES WITH BLOTTING PAPER or paper towels to absorb moisture in damp or musty cupboards.

MUSTY BREADBINS. After washing bin, sprinkle baking soda on bottom of bin and cover with greaseproof paper.

PAPER KITCHEN TOWELS
- Use in place of plates and chopping boards to butter bread or toast, grate vegetables or cheese, or crumb and flour meat and fish. No plates to wash or crumbs to wipe away.

- Wrap around neck of cooking oil bottle, securing tightly with a rubber band. Paper absorbs oily drips.

PLASTIC CARRY BAGS make great liners for a kitchen tidy. When full, tie the handles into a knot and put into your rubbish bag.

CLEAN A VACUUM FLASK by filling with hot water and adding a denture cleaning tablet. Leave overnight, then rinse well.

TO REMOVE STICKY LABELS FROM ICE-CREAM CONTAINERS, fill container with hot water, immerse in hot water and leave until label peels off easily. Rub away sticky residue with metal-polish such as Brasso.

TO CLEAN THE BASE OF A CAPPUCCINO MAKER. Sprinkle dishwasher powder on the base, add hot water, leave for five minutes then wipe down.

USED ALUMINIUM FOIL makes an effective scouring pad for pans and casseroles.

RID A PICKLED ONION JAR of smells by filling with warm water and adding one dessertspoon of baking soda. Leave for a few hours.

CLEAR THE KITCHEN OF FUMES by boiling mint or herbs in an open saucepan containing about a litre of water. Leave windows open.

ROTTEN FOOD SMELLS IN A FREEZER. After an extended period without power the smells in a freezer are tough to remove. Take all contents out of freezer compartment and wash out with a strong solution of baking soda then wash again with a strong disinfectant, following freezer supplier's instructions.

FRIDGE-FREEZER SMELLS
- Wash the inside very thoroughly with malt vinegar, repeating

several times, and then dry.
- Put a cut-up raw onion in the fridge and close the door.

PUT LEMON SKINS IN A SMALL BOWL inside the refrigerator to absorb odours while emitting their own fresh smell.

REMOVE ONION AND GARLIC SMELLS
- Remove smells from chopping boards by making a paste with water and baking soda. Always wash board in cold water first. Cover the board with the paste and leave for a few minutes. Scrub and rinse in cold water.
- To remove onion and garlic from hands, wash in cold water.

AWKWARD-TO-CLEAN KITCHEN UTENSILS such as mincers and egg-beaters can be tackled with a bottle-brush. Also use for hollow-stemmed glasses and narrow vases.

CHAPTER THREE
ALL STEAMED UP
BATHROOM BASICS

Mirrors

CLEAN A BATHROOM MIRROR QUICKLY by wiping with newspaper sheets.

POLISH A MIRROR with talcum powder on a clean cloth.

REMOVE FILM FROM A MIRROR
Apply a thin paste of baking soda and cold water and leave for 15 minutes, then rub off with a soft cloth.
Rub gently with methylated spirit on a steel-wool pad, then polish with a soft, dry cloth.

STOP BATHROOM MIRRORS MISTING UP
- Rub with a clean cloth dipped in glycerine or methylated spirits.
- Rub surface with a cake of soap, then polish with a clean cloth.

The bath

A CURTAIN RING attached to the bath plug will make the plug easier to pull.

DISCOLOURED, SLIMY BATH PLUGS.
- Should be left to stand for a few hours or overnight in a weak

solution of water and bleach in a jar. Wipe inner seal, then rinse well.
- Prevent slimy plugs by wiping regularly when bath or basin is cleaned.

TIDE MARKS IN THE BATH
- Remove stubborn tide marks by washing with a solution of water, vinegar and ammonia.
- Rub around tide marks with turpentine.
- Stop tide marks forming by wiping sides of the bath at water level immediately after a bath.

NO SOAP DISH? Place a damp flannel over the edge of the bath while you're soaking and sit the soap on it. No more fumbling around for the soap in the water!

STAINED ACRYLIC OR FIBREGLASS BATH
- Rub stains with a mixture of lemon juice and salt.
- Gently rub tough stains with fine sandpaper and, when smooth, wipe with silver polish. Rinse well. (Editor's note: Avoid using strong abrasive cleaners on acrylic or fibreglass surfaces.)

STAINED ENAMEL BATH
- Gently rub stains from a dripping tap with a soap scourer pad, or a weak solution of ammonia and soap flakes in warm water. Rinse with clear water and wipe dry.
- If stain is obstinate, fill bath with very hot water, and add water softener as recommended on the packet. Leave until cool enough to handle, then scrub with nylon mesh pad or brush, rinse and rub dry.
- For yellowish, rust-like marks, mix 4 tablespoons flour, 4 tablespoons vinegar and 8 tablespoons diluted hydrogen peroxide into a paste (Note: Wear rubber gloves). Apply to marks, leave a few hours and wash off with cold water.
- Rub stains hard with denture plate powder on a damp cloth. If

a stain is stubborn, mix denture powder to a paste and spread on to marked area. Leave for a few hours, then wash off.
- Rub marks with kerosene on a damp cloth.

The shower

MILDEW ON SHOWER CURTAINS
- Rub mildew marks with baking soda or a mild bleach solution, then rinse in clean water.
- Scrub stains with Swarfega or other cleaning gel, then rinse.
- Soak overnight in a bucket of water with ½ cup of ammonia, then wash as normal.
- Put shower curtain in washing machine with two large bath towels, add ½ cup each of detergent and baking soda and run through wash cycle (check manufacturer's instructions). Add 1 cup of vinegar to rinse water. Do not spin, but hang out immediately.
- Wash nylon curtains once a week in warm, soapy water (follow manufacturer's instructions).
- Stop build-up of mildew on plastic curtains by soaking in bleach solution once a week.
- After washing, hang a plastic curtain sideways on the line to let water drain from hem; or trim hem from curtain.
- Soak a new shower curtain in strong, salty water for 30 minutes before first using.

CREASED PLASTIC CURTAINS.
Run a hot iron over ironing board cover, immediately place plastic curtain over the warm area and smooth out with the hands.

GLASS SHOWER DOORS
- Remove excess water after showering with a rubber window-cleaning scraper.
- Sponge glass with white vinegar.

SOAP SCUM ON GLASS AND TILES
- Rub with baking soda on a wet cloth.
- Make a solution of sugar soap and apply with a coarse cloth (Note: wear rubber gloves) and rinse well.
- Rub with an equal quantity of kerosene and vinegar and polish with a soft dry cloth.
- Rub with white vinegar.

KEEP SHOWER CURTAINS PLIABLE by adding glycerine to the water when rinsing.

Toilet

WASH TOILET BOWL WITH VINEGAR to remove water marks.

NEVER COMBINE TOILET CLEANERS as the results could be toxic.

LIGHT AND BLOW OUT A MATCH to get rid of odours.

KEEP SPARE LOO ROLLS HANDY AND TIDY by storing in a wicker basket or wastebin.

Soap savers

STORE BULK-BUY SOAP with wrappings off. The soap cakes will harden and last longer when used.

REDUCE CRACKS IN SOAP CAKE by turning cracked side down while wet.

USE BULK-BUY FAMILY SHAMPOO as a cheap liquid soap.

LIQUID SOAP RECIPE Add hot water and a little food colouring to soap scraps in a jug. Mix well.

General hints

COTTON BATH TOWELS will come up softer and more absorbent if you interrupt your wash cycle to add a tablespoon of glycerine to the rinsing water.

DRYING OFF. Before stepping out of the bath or shower, use a flannel to give yourself a preliminary dry, wringing out flannel after use. Towel and bath mat will stay drier!

OLD BATH TOWELS can be turned into bath mats if folded in half and sewn together.

MILDEW STAINS ON A NON-SLIP BATH MAT should be covered with lemon juice and the mat left in the sun to dry.

CLEAN BATHROOM FITTINGS with paraffin, applied on a clean cloth.

GENERAL-PURPOSE CLEANER. Make up a spray solution of disinfectant and water in an empty spray-clean bottle.

REMOVE MILDEW FROM GROUTING with a solution of bleach and water.

STIFF SLIDING-DOORS on a bathroom cabinet should be rubbed with vaseline.

TIDY TOOTHPASTE-HOLDER. Place a heavy metal bulldog clip over the bottom end of the tube, and hang it to a hook or nail on the wall. The tube will hang upside down. To disperse paste, remove cap and simply press tube against wall.

USE AN OLD TOOTHBRUSH to clean grouting and difficult crevices.

USING UP TOOTHPASTE
- Stand tube on its cap in hot water for a few minutes. Extra paste comes out easily.
- Cut off top and bottom of tube and split open. Wrap in plastic to prevent paste drying. (Useful for hand lotion, face cream, etc – anything that comes in a tube.)

CHAPTER FOUR

SOAP SUDS & GLORY

LAUNDRY LORE

In the wash

ANTI-STATIC REMEDY FOR SYNTHETICS. Spray with a mixture of 1.5 cups fabric softener and 2 cups water when ironing.

AUTOMATIC WASHING MACHINE SMELLS. After use, leave washing machine lid fully or partly up to eliminate musty smell caused by lack of air.

BLACK CLOTHES WON'T FADE if a few drops of vinegar are put into washing water.

BLANKET FRAGRANCE. For a pleasant smell, add a dissolved bathcube to the rinsing water when washing blankets.

CEMENT ON CLOTHING can be removed by adding a cup of vinegar to a bucket of water and soaking overnight.

CHIFFON SCARF CARE. Hand wash then dip scarf into a thin solution of plastic starch or a teaspoon of unflavoured gelatine dissolved in 500ml water. Iron when dry.

DARK CLOTHES should be washed inside out to stop them picking up fluff from other clothes.

DO UP ZIPS, BUTTONS AND BELTS before putting clothes in

washing machine, to avoid tangling.

FEATHER DUVET CARE
- Feathers (unlike kapok or wool) wash and dry well. To clean the whole duvet, wash it in the bath with warm, soapy water. Drain the water away and rinse twice in clear, warm water; choose a windy day to dry outdoors, turning the duvet often to prevent feathers from settling in one end.
- If you prefer, spot cleaning can be used. A commercial solvent, if rubbed on outside of duvet, will not harm the feathers. Treated patch can be washed afterwards if desired, and dried as usual. (Editor's note: Always use a commercial solvent out of doors, and do not inhale the fumes.)

GLOVES CAN BE WASHED while they are on your hands. Much quicker!

INVERT A SAUCER OVER THE SINK PLUG when handwashing clothes. The plug is less likely to be bumped out of place.

LIQUID SOAP RECIPES
- Place small scraps of toilet soap into empty liquid soap container until about quarter full, then pour in hot water till about three-quarters full and give it a good shake. Leave for a day or so till soft and runny. If too thick, add more hot water and mix.
- Shred enough soap scraps to fill a 600ml jug, add 600ml of boiling water and 1 tablespoon borax and stir until dissolved. Pour into dispenser jar.

MAKE TOWELS MORE ABSORBENT
- Boil towels in detergent in a large saucepan or boiler.
- Soak overnight in cold water to which 1 tablespoon of epsom salts has been added. Wash as usual after soaking. Plain coloured towels should be soaked separately.
- Add fabric softener to the wash.

NAPPY CARE. Always soak nappies in cold water before washing. Do not use too much soap or powder or detergent or the nappies will go slightly pink. Impregnating the material with lots of soap is not only unnecessary for cleanliness but will cause a rash quicker than anything. Rinse thoroughly to get all the soap out.

NEVER WRING OUT STARCHED GARMENTS. Slide them through hands, squeezing all the time. Hang garments on the line quite wet. Dry completely, then dampen before ironing.

NEW SHEETS THAT ARE TOO STIFF TO USE
- Add ½ cup turpentine to water when washing sheets. After rinsing, hang them out to dry. No smell of turpentine will remain.
- Place sheets in a tub of cold water and add 50g epsom salts. Agitate sheets for two minutes, then leave overnight. Rinse in fresh water and hang to dry.
- Add two handfuls of salt to cold water and soak sheets overnight.
- Dissolve 6 tablespoons borax in a tub of cold water and soak sheets overnight. Next morning rinse thoroughly in cold water and hang out to dry.

NEW WORK OVERALLS. Wash before use, then apply some starch. This prevents oil etc. soaking into the material.

OLD RECIPE FOR WATERPROOFING BOOTS
Take 50g resin, 50g beeswax, 50g mutton fat (free of salt) and 250ml linseed oil. Heat until wax is melted, not letting mixture get too hot, then apply with a soft cloth and rub in well.

ORANGE-COLOURED STAINS ON NAPPIES
- Work a few drops of glycerine into stains. Leave overnight, then dampen with a few drops of white vinegar and wash nappies out with warm water after two minutes.
- If soaking nappies in one of the enzyme powders available has

failed, cover stains with lemon juice and leave nappies in fresh air for several hours. Rinse in cold water then wash as usual.
- Hang nappies in strong sunshine to bleach out stains naturally.

PIN SOCKS TOGETHER IN PAIRS before putting them in the wash. No more odd socks!

PLACE KNITWEAR IN A PILLOWCASE to prevent it stretching in the wash.

REVITALISE WOOLLENS with a tablespoon of glycerine added to washing and rinsing water.

SET COLOURS IN SILK. Dissolve packet of epsom salts in cold water and rinse garment before washing for the first time in warm water.

SHINE ON TROUSERS
Dip stiff nail brush in 500ml warm water which contains one dessertspoon ammonia. Shake surplus water off thoroughly and brush garment. Avoid making it too wet. Dry on a hanger in the open air, and press as usual.

SOAK DIRTY OVERALLS in warm water containing a little ammonia, then wash as normal.

STOP A SWEATER FROM STRETCHING when handwashing by rinsing it in a colander and gently squeezing out the excess water.

TO WASH A WHITE SHEEPSKIN RUG make a good lather with white soap and ammonia and give rug a good soaking, working it round and round. Rinse once or twice in clean water. In the final water, put 1 tablespoon borax. Never use harsh detergents.

TO WATERPROOF FABRICS use a solution of 1 teaspoon gum arabic, 2 tablespoons vinegar and 1 cup warm water. Mix together well and brush on with a stiff brush. Test on a small piece of the material first, as synthetic fibres may not take the solution satisfactorily.

TOYS WITH SEWN-ON CLOTHES
- Sprinkle toys with fuller's earth (obtainable at hardware and paint shops) or powdered magnesia. Rub in gently with tips of fingers, roll toys up in paper. Leave overnight. Next day, take the toys outside and gently beat them with your hand to remove loose powder.
- Sprinkle with bran moistened with hot water. Dry with a face flannel or similar. Rub with a fresh cloth and some dry bran. Shake toys afterwards, to remove all surplus bran.
- A carpet shampoo also might do the job. Remember to keep a dry cloth always on the go, mopping up the shampoo as you work, so that the article doesn't become damp.
- Spray thoroughly with a can of spray-on dry-cleaning preparation, then vacuum well, using the nozzle provided with your cleaner for vacuuming upholstery.

USE EMPTY PLASTIC DISHWASH POWDER BOTTLES for storing ordinary washing powders. The powder stays dry and free of lumps.

WASH SWEATERS IN SHAMPOO for a soft finish.

WASHING INSTRUCTION LABELS. After removing the care instruction label to keep for later reference, write on it a description of garment it belongs to.

Drying tips

TO ATTACH COATHANGER TO WASHING LINE
- Fold a rubber preserving jar ring over line and pull one half

tightly through the other. Hang coat hanger on loop.
- Drill holes through the two prongs of a clothes peg, attach to line, then slip the coathanger hook through the holes, where it will be held fast.

CLOTHES PEGS WILL HOLD BETTER on a windy day if they are put in at an angle rather than upright.

DRY A CANDLEWICK BEDCOVER on the line with the tufted sides together. The tufts rub against each other and fluff themselves up, especially if they are hung in a good wind.

KEEP FLIES AWAY FROM A CLOTHESLINE
- Peg plastic bags or sheets of clear plastic at intervals between clothes on the line. The movement and rustling noise of the plastic keeps flies away.
- Spray the ground around clothesline with a strong disinfectant.

MAKE A STAND FOR DRYING JERSEYS and other woollen garments by removing the top from an old folding table and replacing it with wire netting. When not in use, the stand is easily stowed away.

PLACE SHOULDER PADS INSIDE WOOLLENS when drying to prevent stretching and ugly coathanger marks.

SEW TAPES TO CORNERS OF A THICK BATH MAT for easy pegging on the line after washing.

STOP SHEETS WRAPPING THEMSELVES AROUND A CLOTHESLINE on windy days by pegging both ends of sheet to the line and slipping a sealed plastic bottle, half-filled with water, in the fold. A 1.5 litre drink bottle is ideal.

T-SHIRTS DRY MORE QUICKLY on a line if air can circulate between the front and back.

WASHING LINE SPACE-SAVER. Peg clothes out so that they are suspended between two lines rather than along each one.

Ironing

BEDSPREADS CAN BE IRONED on their beds rather than on an ironing board. No folding!

FILL A STEAM IRON SAFELY using an indoor watering can with a long narrow spout.

REMOVE CREASES FROM LACE NETTING by boiling the jug and holding the netting over the steam until creases disappear.

CHECK THE THERMOSTAT ON AN IRON if it is constantly scorching.

LIGHTLY SCORCHED COTTON OR WOOLLENS.
- If scorched while ironing, rub garment immediately with the edge of a piece of silver money, then rub with the flat surface.
- Rub surface gently with a very fine sandpaper.

IRONING MADE EASIER. Place aluminium foil under ironing board cover to reflect heat and increase efficiency.

NO TIME FOR IRONING!
- Dampen clothes, place them in a plastic bag and put in the refrigerator.
- Put small amounts of near-dry or even fully dry washing in the tumble drier at a moderate heat for a few minutes. Takes creases out of most garments and some linen.

SOILED ELECTRIC IRON
- Run warm iron over brown paper on which salt has been sprinkled.

- Rub rhubarb leaf over iron base.
- While iron is still warm, rub the plate with a dry steel soap pad until all the residue is removed.

UNBLEACHED CALICO contains chemicals which scorch easily when ironed, so wash unbleached material before making an ironing board cover with it.

Shoe cleaning tips

TO SOFTEN LUMPY SHOE POLISH
- Stand polish tin on a low heat until completely melted. Leave to cool and set.
- Put some baby oil in it and leave for a while in the hot water cupboard.
- Add a little methylated spirits to polish. Blend with a blunt knife blade.
- Put a few drops of methylated spirits on top of polish, rub with old newspaper and then polish shoes with newspaper.
- Put some kerosene into the tin, place on warm stove until lumps are melted, then shift carefully and let contents set. (Editor's note: use low heat only to heat polish, or heat by standing tin in water.)

BLACK MARKS ON SHOES. Rub with a little Brasso on a cloth. Use a damp cloth first, then a dry one. This method also takes tar off shoes or from inside your car.

TO SOFTEN A PAIR OF PIGSKIN SHOES
- Rub in castor oil, leave for 48 hours, then polish.
- Buy a small tin of dubbin or neats' foot oil from a saddlery and apply as instructed.

SCUFF MARKS ON SHOES Rub shoes gently with eucalyptus oil.

WHITE LEATHER SHOES. Brush on Twink correction fluid to cover rubbed patches.

Smells

FISHY SMELLS ON VELVET
- If fabric is washable, add one teaspoon of dry mustard to final rinse.
- Wash fabric gently in warm water, using a cake of white, perfumed toilet soap. Rinse twice in warm water, adding half a cup of household vinegar to the final rinse.
- Use a good spray-on fabric deodoriser obtainable from a chemist. It is stronger than ordinary air deodorisers.

TO FRESHEN SMELLY SHOES sprinkle inside with baking soda, leave for several hours or overnight before dusting out.

REMOVE THE SMELL OF CAT URINE from a pair of sneakers or running shoes, by placing shoes in plastic bag with a handful of baking soda. Tie the bag and shake thoroughly, leave for at least four days, remove shoes, shake out all the powder, and place in sunlight for a day.

TO REMOVE THE SMELL OF DIESEL FUMES FROM CLOTHING
- Soak in a bucket of water containing ¼ cup household ammonia. Make sure the bucket is out of children's reach.
- Soak in warm water containing two or three tablespoons of baking soda.
- Mix one tablespoon of dry mustard with a little cold water and add to a bucket of cold water and soak garment overnight.
- Sprinkle garment liberally with dry mustard, roll up and secure in a plastic bag overnight, then wash.

TANNING SMELL ON A SUEDE JACKET. Sponge very lightly on

wrong side only with vinegar, which is a neutraliser, then brush with suede brush. Smell will lessen in time. (Hang jacket outdoors in the shade as much as possible.)

RESTORE SOFTNESS AND COLOUR TO OLD KID GLOVES by pulling gloves on hands and rubbing olive oil well into kid, a few drops at a time, until you have gone over each glove thoroughly. (For dark shades.)

DIRTY LEATHER JACKET COLLAR
- To clean, use a good leather soap cleaner from the saddlers. Wring a cloth out of warm water, apply a little soap and rub on. Sponge clean with more water, and dry off. Polish with a good shoe cream.
- Rub neckline with a soft cloth dampened with eucalyptus. When dry, wipe a little petroleum jelly over the area and after a while polish with a soft cloth. (Editor's note: Test in an inconspicuous place on collar first.)

TRAVELLING LAUNDRY BAG. Using safety pins, attach one side of an open pillow slip to a wire coathanger and hang bag on any convenient peg.

FLUFF ON DARK CLOTHING
- Wrap a strip of sticky tape around hand, sticky side out, and dab it over clothing.
- Brush in one direction with a piece of dry foam sponge.

ITCHY WOOLLEN JUMPER. Place in a plastic bag in the freezer overnight.

CHAPTER FIVE
ELBOW GREASE & VINEGAR
CLEANING UP

ALUMINIUM WINDOW FRAMES. Use an old toothbrush to clean dust and dirt from the moulded crevices.

ANIMAL HAIRS ON CARPETS AND FURNITURE. Remove by wiping over with a sponge dampened with a little vinegar and water.

BLACK BOOT SKID-MARKS on rubber tiles will disappear if rubbed gently with a wire soap pad.

BRIGHTEN PAINTWORK by melting a few tablespoons of painter's size in boiling water. When cooled, wring out a cloth in the solution and clean the paintwork with it. Dries to a fine shine.

CARPET STATIC can be treated by putting some fabric softener into a small bottle with water (about one part softener to four parts water), shaking well and misting the carpet with this.

CHIMNEY SOOT ON CARPETS should be vacuumed up immediately. Never dampen the area as this will cause a grimy stain.

CHINA CABINET CARE
- Wipe cabinet out thoroughly with a damp rag dipped in vinegar, and leave door open to dry. Repeat if necessary. Wash china very well and leave out of the cabinet until odour has gone.

- Wash all china well, then put a few grains of permanganate of potash in a bowl of water and leave in the cabinet for a day or two. Remove, and after replacing china, put a piece of coke in each corner of cabinet. This will keep it fresh.
- Leave a mint leaf in the cabinet.
- Wash shelves of cabinet and teaset with warm water in which a handful of baking soda has been dissolved.
- Add a few dry tea leaves to the teapot stored with a tea set in a cabinet to keep it fresh.
- Air cabinet thoroughly at regular intervals.

CLEAN MARBLE by adding a little turpentine to some lukewarm water. Apply with a cloth, then polish with a soft duster.

CHROME SURFACES can be polished with nail polish remover. Rinse well with water.

DIP A PIPECLEANER IN METAL POLISH to clean between the prongs of a fork.

DUST SILK FLOWERS with a hair drier, or brush with a slightly dampened toothbrush.

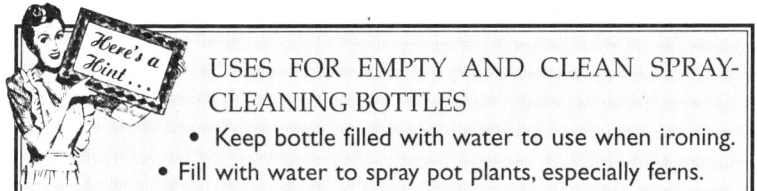

USES FOR EMPTY AND CLEAN SPRAY-CLEANING BOTTLES
- Keep bottle filled with water to use when ironing.
- Fill with water to spray pot plants, especially ferns.
- Fill with pot plant fertiliser.

ECONOMICAL FURNITURE POLISH.
Mix two parts castor oil with one part camphorated oil. Polish has a pleasant smell.

FINGERMARKS ON POLISHED FURNITURE. Wipe over with a

cloth dipped in vinegar and water then rub with furniture polish in normal way.

FLATTENED PILE ON VELVET CURTAINS
- Spin in the spin-drier for 20 minutes. The warmth and the spinning action will bring the pile up.
- Hang curtains in the bathroom while you are having a bath or shower, and let the steam permeate them. Brush gently with a soft brush and leave to dry thoroughly before rehanging.
- Boil a jug of water near where curtains hang to steam them, then vacuum, using upholstery attachment and concentrating on the marked area.

FLOOR POLISH RECIPES
- Melt 75g shredded beeswax and 60g soap flakes in warmed water. When dissolved, remove from heat, add 250ml turpentine and 250ml kerosene. Stir occasionally until cold. Add lavender oil for a fresh scent.
- Cut small pieces of beeswax and cover with turpentine, put aside until softened, then stir until well mixed.
- Mix together 55g of shellac, 55g of resin and 1 litre of methylated spirits. Shake well till shellac and resin are dissolved. Wipe over linoleum and leave to dry.
- Mix together equal quantities of turpentine and kerosene. This is a good disinfectant and leaves a shiny, non-slip polish.

FLY SPECKS ON MIRRORS AND WINDOWS come off if rubbed with equal parts of vinegar and water.

FOR A DUSTLESS DUSTER, soak a piece of cheesecloth or cotton in kerosene. Hang out to dry, then keep in a tin with a lid.

HIGH GLOSS ON STAINLESS STEEL. Apply powdered whiting on a damp sponge, allow to dry, then polish.

CLEAN VENETIAN blinds with water containing a little kerosene.

KEROSENE IN cleaning water acts as a fly repellent.

MILDEW ON THERMAL DRAPES should be brushed with a stiff brush and the drapes then sponged with white vinegar. The vinegar odour will soon disappear. (Test in an inconspicuous area.)

MUSTY CUPBOARDS
- Ensure air gets in. For tight-fitting cupboards, bore 1cm holes in a triangle at one corner of the door, barely visible if the edges of the holes are neatly sandpapered.
- Thoroughly scrub insides of cupboards with baking soda and hot water. Leave doors open so that drying is total. Leave a small saucer of lime on each shelf to maintain freshness.
- Tip a small packet of baking soda into a large basin, fill with hot water, stir well and place in the cupboard. Leave for several days.
- Leave a cut lemon in the cupboard for a few days.
- Scrub cupboards out with warm water and ammonia. When quite dry, spray out with an air freshener. Leave doors open for several hours. Spray again, if needed.

OLD-FASHIONED CUT-GLASS VASES
- Three-quarters fill vase with warm water, add some washing powder and a generous amount of bleach and allow to stand for 30 minutes or more.
- Put dry denture cleaning powder into the vase, top up with hot water and let stand a couple of hours.
- Always wash vase immediately after use in warm water and washing soda.
- Fill with a household bleach solution every couple of weeks and leave for a few hours to clean.

PAINTED WOODWORK can be cleaned by rubbing with a mixture of methylated spirits and kerosene. Finish with a soft clean duster.

> **USES FOR VINEGAR**
> - As a glass polisher: moisten a cloth in the vinegar, rub well into the glass, and polish with a clean dry cloth.
> - To remove fingermarks from wooden furniture: wipe down with a cloth dampened in vinegar.

PAINTWORK STAYS CLEAN after washing if rubbed with silicone furniture polish when dry.

PARQUET, POLISHED WOOD AND CORK FLOORS. Clean with a damp sponge with a little mineral turps on it. When dry, buff up. Apply liquid polish once a fortnight.

PICTURE FRAME GLASS should be cleaned with methylated spirits, as this evaporates quickly. Apply with a paper tissue, then polish with a dry tissue. Never use a cloth dampened with water, as the moisture may seep through to the frame and stain the picture or the mount.

POLISH BUILD-UP ON FURNITURE. Rub with brown vinegar on a damp cloth and polish with a duster.

PREVENT CHAMOIS LEATHER FROM STIFFENING WHEN DRY
- Wash in very lathery warm water, using pure soapflakes. Rinse in clean, warm water and wash once more in a rich, pure soap lather, but do not rinse again. Dry away from direct heat. The secret lies in not rinsing out the soap.
- Wash chamois in warm water containing a little ammonia, and do not wring it out before drying. While chamois is drying, work it with hands occasionally to keep it soft. Dry in a shady place.
- Add a little glycerine or olive oil to the last rinsing water to keep chamois leather pliable.

PUT AN OLD SOCK ON YOUR HAND to clean venetian blinds.

RECIPES FOR WINDOW CLEANER SPIRITS
- Place 1 cup methylated spirits, 1 cup water (hot), 1 cup kerosene in a screw-top bottle and shake well. Apply to windows or glass with damp cloth.
- Put a dab of hair shampoo in a small amount of water. Rub on any glass surface and rub off excess moisture with a clean cloth.

REFRESH LEATHER FURNITURE
Mix 2 tablespoons of turpentine, 1 teaspoon of linseed oil and the lightly beaten whites of two eggs. Apply to leather with a soft, clean cloth.

REMOVE STICKY LABELS FROM FURNITURE by spraying with a pre-wash stain remover. Leave for a few minutes, then wipe away.

RESTORE OLD LINO by rubbing with linseed oil.

TO RID MATTRESS OF URINE SMELL
- Wipe with a solution of equal parts vinegar and warm water, then air in the sun. Use two or three applications.
- Sponge lightly with water containing one tablespoon baking soda, then sprinkle liberally with baking soda powder. Repeat if necessary.

RUB OLD BONE-HANDLED KNIVES with lemon juice or a paste of cream of tartar to whiten yellowed handles.

RUB WINDOWS with a freshly cut potato, then wipe dry, for a streak-free clean.

SALT SPRAY MARKS ON WINDOWS. Remove by dipping a cloth in dry flour and rubbing. Polish with a soft dry cloth.

STAINED LINO TREATMENT. Rub stain with turpentine or kerosene, then wash and polish lightly.

STICKY LABEL RESIDUE ON GLASS comes off if sprayed with WD40.

STOP FLOWER WATER FROM SMELLING
- Put a small piece of charcoal into the vase with the flowers.
- Remove leaves from below the point where the stalks enter the water to stop leaves rotting in the water.
- Change the water frequently, and after emptying dead flowers wash vase in warm, soapy water.

THERMAL DRAPES. If the back appears to stick together slightly after washing, sprinkle talcum powder lightly over and rub it in gently.

THERMAL SULPHUR DEPOSITS ON WINDOWS
- Dip a rolled wet newspaper into fireplace ashes and rub over windows. Wash off with hose or buckets of clean water.
- Add 8 drops of brass cleaner to half a bucket of warm water. Wipe on window and rub with a dry cloth.

USE BOTTLE CORKS TO CLEAN GLASS. Rubbed over surface spots of windows or mirrors, they clean instantly without a cleaning agent. Rub glass with a soft cloth for a final polish.

VARNISHED WOOD cleans up well if rubbed with cold tea on a cloth.

WASH DECORATIVE CANDLES which have become soiled in cool, soapy water. Remove quickly and dry with a soft cloth.

WHEN WASHING WINDOWS ON THE INSIDE keep curtains out of the way by tucking them through clothes hangers and hanging them from the curtain rod.

WINDOWS AND MIRRORS come up clean and streak-free if rubbed with scrunched up, damp newspaper.

WIPE SMEARY WINDOWS with a wad of old pantihose after cleaning.

WOODEN HAIRBRUSHES are best smeared with a little vaseline or petroleum jelly before washing, to protect the wood from the water.

YELLOWING IVORY PIANO KEYS
- Wipe keys with methylated spirits.
- Rub with toothpaste on a soft cloth.

Jewellery care

CLEAN DIAMOND RINGS AND GOLD JEWELLERY with a little toothpaste on a soft damp cloth or soft toothbrush. Rub gently, dunk in warm water, rinse and polish with a soft cloth.

RUB GOLD JEWELLERY between your hands with fresh breadcrumbs to make it shine.

JEWELLERY CLEANER
Immerse in warm mixture of baking soda and water, move item around and dirt floats off.

ANTIQUE BROOCH. To prevent jewellery from leaving dark stains on skin and clothing, wash in hot soapy water to which liquid ammonia has been added in a ratio of one part ammonia to nine parts water. Rinse in clear water. Rub with a soft dry cloth. Place in open container and leave in hotwater cupboard for a couple of hours to dry thoroughly. Finally, coat back of jewellery with clear nail varnish .

Cleaning brass, copper and silver

POLISHING TIPS
- Solid copper: rub with a mixture of common salt and vinegar.

JEWELLERY TREATMENTS

- Gold, platinum and silver: in soapy, luke-warm water, dry with a soft cotton cloth and polish with clean chamois.
- Gems set in silver or gold: Dip into warm soapy water, rinse in cold water, then polish.
- Diamonds: Rinse in cold water and when dry polish with chamois. A few drops of pure alcohol on the backs will make them sparkle.
- Turquoise: Spirits and moisture are harmful, just polish with a soft cloth.
- Opals: Hot water is harmful and will sometimes crack them. Polish with whiting, rinse in cold water and rub dry.
- Pearls: Place in powdered magnesia for a few hours shake away the powder and polish gently with a soft cloth.
- Jet: Remove all dust. Moisten a cloth with warm olive oil, rub the jet lightly then polish with chamois. Because it is so brittle, jet needs careful handling.
- Ivory: Must not be washed in soapy water or it will turn yellow. Rub lightly with baking soda dissolved in warm water. If ivory has yellowed, wipe it with a soft cloth moistened with peroxide of hydrogen and place it in the sun to whiten.
- Sapphires and rubies: Dip a soft toothbrush in boiled water containing detergent and dab at stones. Buff with a soft cloth.
- Emeralds: Avoid cleaning these yourself as they break easily.
- Cameos and jade: Wash in cold water, clean with a soft brush and smear lightly with olive oil.

For copper-plated articles use a commercial metal-polish, but read the instructions.

- Dull or tarnished brass (solid brass, not plated): rub with a cloth dipped in kerosene or a methylated spirits cleaner, then scrub with warm water and detergent. Rinse with water, dry, then shine up with metal-polish.
- Plated brassware: use commercial metal-polish, or you may

remove some of the plating.
- Pewter: rub over with dry flour on a dry cloth.
- Silver: use commercial silver-polish such as Silvo. If item is valuable, consult jeweller for care instructions.

татем TO CLEAN BRASS ORNAMENTS use a mixture of 1 cup vinegar and 2 tablespoons salt, with enough flour to thicken. Non-lacquered brass can be cleaned with a paste of fine whiting and linseed oil, then dipped in hot soapsuds and polished with a chamois leather.

TO CLEAN COPPER, soak a while in water to which a teaspoon of cream of tartar has been added. Rinse off.

SILVER CLEANER.
Mix a paste from three parts baking soda to one part of water. Apply with a damp sponge, rinse off and polish.

TREAT BRASS ORNAMENTS WITH LEMON JUICE applied with an old soft toothbrush. Wash ornaments in warm, soapy water.

CHAPTER SIX
POTTING & PAINT
GARDENING & DIY

Gardening

A LARGE THICK PLASTIC BAG half-filled with soil and peat is ideal for storing bulbs, plants, etc, outdoors until you have time to plant them in the garden. Fold the top of the bag over to prevent dirt getting too wet. If it rains, leave enough of an opening for air to circulate. This is a good start for frost-tender plants.

AN OLD LADDER makes a good support for a rambler rose or similar plant.

AS A PROTECTIVE UMBRELLA when setting out flower plants, gather small branches from shrubs and push one of these in the ground beside each plant. Remove when plants have rooted.

BEFORE GOING ON HOLIDAY remove spent blooms from flowers and shrubs; this will encourage more growth.

BOILED EGG WATER, once cool, is a good source of minerals for your house plants.

BURY OLD STEEL WOOL SCOURERS under hydrangea bushes to intensify blue flowers.

BUY GARDEN SEEDS IN BULK as an economy measure and share with friends.

CARDBOARD MILK CARTONS, tops removed, make good seed-trays.

CHRISTMAS TREE CARE. Before putting tree in its display tub, stand it overnight in a bucket of cold water in which two disprin have been dissolved.

CRUMPLE ALUMINIUM FOIL into the bottom of a vase. Arrange flowers, punching stems through foil. Flowers stay fresher and the water keeps clean for longer.

CURLY LEAF ON PEACH TREES. Mix 1kg of epsom salts in a little hot water to dissolve, add cold water to make up 10 litres. Let cool then pour on ground around trees, from outside branches to within 25 cm of trees. The above amount would do one very large tree or two smaller ones. Repeat two or three times a year.

CUT FLOWERS STAY FRESH if you add a little salt, an aspirin or a small block of camphor to the water in which the flowers are arranged.

DIG A HOLE BELOW THE GARDEN TAP and fill it with gravel. Any drips will drain away instead of forming a quagmire or fostering a crop of weeds.

FLORAL DISPLAY IN WINTER. When flowers are scarce, tuck a spray from an azalea or other shrub in with a leafy pot-plant.

FLOWERS ARE EASIER TO RAISE FROM SEEDS than most people realise and this is much cheaper than buying plants. Mix equal parts of potting mix and fine garden soil. Place in small troughs and sow seeds as directed on packet. Keep troughs in the hot-water cupboard, moistening them gently every two or three days until the tiny plants have appeared. They can then be kept on a window-sill or other warm place until ready to plant.

FLOWERS LAST LONGER if picked first thing in the morning, or in the evening.

GARDEN-SOILED HANDS
- Mix a spoonful of sugar with a little butter or soap and rub.
- Keep soap scraps in an old stocking next to the garden tap.

GARDENING GLOVES. When cotton gloves make fiddly garden jobs difficult, keep hands warm with surgical gloves purchased from a chemist.

GARLIC PLANTED BETWEEN ROSE BUSHES deters aphids.

GREENFLY AND APHIDS. Spray with water in which rhubarb leaves have been steeped.

IMPROMPTU CUTTING COLLECTION. Keep some Oasis in a container in the car boot. When you take a cutting, wet Oasis thoroughly and push cuttings into it for easy transport home.

KEEP GARDEN HOSE IN SHAPE by placing two stakes in the ground and winding the hose around these. Keeps it tidy and tangle-free.

KEEPING BIRDS AWAY
- Grapevines: Just before they start to colour, tie each separate bunch of grapes in a section of discarded nylon stocking or pantihose. Be sure to tie both ends of each piece of stocking, and cut out the very small or damaged grapes before putting on protective covering. Grapes will take a few weeks longer to ripen this way, but they are thoroughly protected from birds, wasps, ants and spiders.
- Newly planted vegetables: Drill hole in bottom of empty aluminium drinks cans for drainage, then thread strong string through the tabs and hang over the garden.
- Fruit trees: Hang small mirrors in branches.

GARDEN SECRETS

We all have our own little ways when gardening. I had a group of mates laughing at my methods a while back, but they didn't laugh when they saw my wonderful vegetable garden.

When my potatoes are beginning to come through I sprinkle sawdust along the rows and it not only keeps slugs and snails off, it stops the birds pecking the sweet shoots.

I plant cabbage, cauliflower and any brassica with a small piece of rhubarb each side of the stalk and never have the clubroot so many growl about.

Carrot seeds are planted in a furrow with a dusting of Cold Water Surf powder and there is never any carrot fly.

I plant parsnips on moistened toilet paper – it helps germination – and I have a bountiful crop of parsnips.

I've done this for many years and hardly ever have to buy vegetables.
Gardener, New Plymouth

LEMON WEDGES IN FLOWERBEDS keep cats out of the garden.

LETTUCES LAST LONGER IN THE GARDEN if one or two leaves from each plant are picked as they begin to form hearts. When picking lettuce hearts, leave three or four lower outside leaves attached to the plant and small lettuces will regrow.

MILDEW-FREE GOOSEBERRIES. Plant chives under gooseberry bushes to deter mildew.

MOPING MAIDENHAIR
- Place about four egg-shells (left over from boiled eggs) in a jar, cover with cold water, screw on lid, leave for two weeks, then add a little of the liquid to the fern. It should soon be healthy and green again.
- Established ferns should be given an occasional weak dose of

sulphate of ammonia – one teaspoon to each 4.5 litres of water.
- Cut off all withered and brown fronds. Water each day with ½ cup of cold tea (free of tea leaves). If a large plant, give a whole cupful.
- Cut up the skin of a banana and mix it with the top soil.
- To keep maidenhair fern in a vase, submerge fern under water for 12 hours, shake well and place it in a vase.

OLD NET CURTAINS placed over red currant bushes and strawberry plants protect the ripe fruit from the birds. Hold in place with clip-on plastic pegs.

ONIONS STORED FOR WINTER can be prevented from sprouting if the dry roots are burnt over a flame.

OUTDOOR POT PLANTS don't have to get waterlogged in very wet weather. Turn the saucer upside down and stand the pot on top. This raises the pot off the ground and allows excess water to drain away.

PADDED GARDENING TROUSERS. Sew a large pocket on each knee of an old pair of trousers and insert a wad of foam rubber in each to protect knees when gardening.

PARSNIP SEEDS. To give them a good start, pour boiling water over the seeds when planting.

PLANT INDIVIDUAL SEEDLINGS in empty toilet rolls. Fill with soil, plant a seed in each and stand upright in a tray. Cardboard biodegrades in soil when transplanted.

PLANT SUNFLOWERS BETWEEN FRUIT TREES. The birds will then eat the sunflower seeds and leave the fruit alone.

PLASTIC PICNIC KNIVES make useful garden tools, especially when repotting plants.

> **Here's a Hint...** Somewhere I read that birds dislike feathers, so I collected some, made a few little "birds" and hung them on the fig tree. It truly works!

PRESERVE FLOWERS BY WAXING. Melt some paraffin (candle) wax and allow to stand for five minutes before pouring into a fairly tall container. Dip flowers in wax for a split second then shake and hang up to dry. The drying process takes only a matter of minutes.

PREVENT LEAF CURL IN STONE FRUIT TREES
- Plant nasturtium plants around trunks.
- Hang seaweed on branches.

PUMPKINS
- Never harvest until they are thoroughly ripe, when the vines have withered and the stems are dry. Cut with stems attached, and leave in the sun for a few days before storing. The stems must be left on, as rot always sets in where a stem is missing.
- Store pumpkins on a shed roof. They get all the sun, and the rain does not affect them, as the slope of the roof drains all the water away. Leave plenty of space between them for the air to circulate.

REPOTTING SMALL PLANTS. Wrap a small piece of wet newspaper around roots, place in pot and cover with soil. This prevents the roots from drying out and, when later planted in the garden, the newspaper will turn into compost.

RETAIN A FLOWER ARRANGEMENT IN PLACE for longer by putting a layer of wet sand in the base of the vase. Keep moist.

RHUBARB LEAVES keep garden tools clean and rust-free. Wipe tools with leaf before putting away. Works on motor-mowers too.

SAUCER FOR AN INDOOR POT PLANT. Put a plastic shower cap over the bottom of the pot when watering.

SEED CONTAINERS. Cardboard milk and cream cartons are ideal containers for growing seeds and cuttings in. When seedlings are ready, cut off bottom of carton and plant in the garden without disturbing roots.

SELF-WATERING HOUSE PLANTS. Before going on holiday, thoroughly soak pot plants then place pots in plastic bags and seal tightly. Place near a window but not in direct sunlight.

SLUGS AND SNAILS
- Catch and drown in a glass of beer left overnight in the garden.
- Sprinkle bran on the ground. Slugs love it but it kills them.
- Into a large container such as a kerosene tin put sawdust or wood-shavings, and approximately 4.5 litres of car sump oil. Mix well. Sprinkle around young cabbage, lettuce, etc.
- Keep slug and snail pellets away from pets by placing pellets inside a length of terracotta piping in the garden.

STOP WEEDS GROWING THROUGH CRACKS IN CONCRETE by putting plain salt in the cracks then taking a jug of boiling water and pouring this on the salt.

TEST WHETHER HOUSE PLANTS NEED WATERING by rapping the side of each pot with the knuckles. If it rings rather than making a dull thud, then it's time to get out the watering can.

THINNING OUT GARDEN PLANTS. Put unwanted plants on kerbside with a notice: "Free plants". Other gardeners will snap them up!

TOMATO PLANT STAKES should be set in groups of four, the tops tied together, wigwam style. Stakes placed in this way will not blow down even in very windy weather.

TO SPREAD LAWN FERTILISER, use a small, empty plastic plant pot with drainage holes.

TIE UP DELICATE PLANTS WITH ELASTIC THREAD. It gives them some freedom while keeping them steady.

WATER HANGING BASKETS without drips by placing ice cubes on top of the soil.

WEEDS can be sprayed without harming plants if you push the spray nozzle through a cross-cut in the bottom of a large empty plastic drink bottle. Place neck of bottle over weed and spray directly.

WHEN GATHERING VEGETABLES from the garden, always go furthest away from the house on fine days; then you won't feel quite so guilty collecting those nearest the house when it is raining.

WIND-BLOWN CHRYSANTHEMUMS. Make a strong support for chrysanthemums with garden netting. Cut a suitable length of netting, tie string to four corners, then fasten string to a fence or stakes. Air gets through the mesh and the support sways with the wind-tossed plants, while giving good support.

DIY

AN OLD TOAST RACK covered with paint makes an ideal letter holder.

BEFORE DRIVING NAILS INTO WOOD, dip them into melted paraffin or soap. Prevents wood from splitting.

BURN LETTERS AND PAPERS without an incinerator by placing paper in a cardboard box with the lid on. Dig a hole in the garden away from the house and place box in it. Contents will burn without blowing all over the garden.

CAR OIL ON CONCRETE
- Sprinkle patch of oil with detergent powder and leave overnight. Sweep or wash off next day.
- Spread dry cement fairly thickly over oil and grease and leave two days before sweeping up.
- Cover spots with garden lime and leave for a few days, then brush the lime off. The spots disappear.
- Cover patch of oil and grease with sawdust. Leave for several days, then sweep with a hard broom. Repeat if necessary.

CATCH THE DRIPS OF WATER WHEN WASHING walls or ceilings by cutting the toe off a discarded sock, rolling the sock top several times and slipping onto the wrist.

CHIPS IN BATH, FRIDGE OR WOODWORK can be covered up with white correction fluid.

CRYSTALLISE FLOWERS FOR DECORATION
Dissolve 800g pure alum in 1 litre of soft water. Boil gently in a covered vessel over a moderate heat. Stir all the time. When alum is dissolved, pour solution into a glass jar; when this is almost cold place a stick across the top so that the flowers and leaves to be crystallised can be hung from this. They must be kept immersed for 24 hours and then hung carefully in the shade until thoroughly dry. Pack in boxes until required.

DARKEN A MAHOGANY CABINET and retain the grain without stripping by applying a mixture of $\frac{1}{3}$ cup each of boiled linseed oil (from paint or hardware store) turpentine and vinegar. Shake well before applying with a soft cloth. Wipe dry, then wipe again with another soft cloth.

ELIMINATE THE SMELL OF PAINT when painting indoors by

putting several small bowls of malt vinegar around. In a newly decorated room leave a sliced onion in a bowl of water overnight to remove paint odours.

HUB CAPS. Paint your name and address or telephone number inside each hub cap of your car. If they get detached while you are on the road, some kind person may return them to you!

LEFTOVER PAINT. Trace a line around the outside of the can with some of the paint, to indicate paint level inside. When you are ready to paint again, you know at a glance the colour and amount available.

LIFT LINOLEUM by rolling it up with the pattern facing outwards. The ends won't curl up when the linoleum is put down again.

LINE A PAINT TRAY with cling wrap or a plastic bag before pouring paint in.

LINO IS EASIER TO LAY if it is first unrolled and left for a while in the sun.

MAKE A SMALL WINDOW LOOK BIGGER. Have the curtain rods wider than the window frame so that open curtains rest against the wall not the window.

MOSS AND MOULD ON CONCRETE can be treated with liquid bleach, undiluted. Pour on concrete and spread with an old rag or sponge. Leave for a day or night then brush with a stiff yard broom or scrubbing brush.

TO REMOVE PAINT SPOTS FROM CONCRETE
- Apply paint-remover and scrub with a wire brush.
- Rub spots with coarse sandpaper.
- Pour strong detergent on to spots to soften paint, then scrub with a hard brush.

PAINTING WINDOW FRAMES
- Mix putty with paint the same colour as the frames before puttying windows. Simplifies touching up the frames.
- Line window glass with masking tape and peel off when painting is finished.
- Smear a little petroleum jelly over the glass. After painting, rub off the petroleum with a rag and the paint spots will come away.
- Clean any paint from glass by rubbing with hot vinegar or a cloth dipped in baking soda.

PLASTIC BREAD BAGS LEFT BY THE DOOR for shoe covers will stop mud being tramped through the house if you are coming indoors for something while working outside.

PROTECT GLASSES FROM PAINT DRIPS by covering lenses with cling wrap.

REMOVE STICKERS FROM CAR WINDSCREEN by spraying with window cleaner. Leave for five minutes and rub or scrape off.

REMOVING OLD WALLPAPER.
- Mix up enough flour paste to cover the wall, stirring well into a bucket of very hot water. Cover the walls with this mixture and allow to soak in. You will have plenty of time to scrape the old paper off before the mixture dries.
- Immerse paint-roller in warm, soapy water and roll over the old paper as if painting.

SET A RUBBISH BAG INSIDE AN OLD CAR TYRE to keep it upright in strong winds.

SOFTEN HARD PAINT BRUSHES by putting them in an old tin with vinegar and a little soap powder. Bring to boil, then rinse thoroughly in warm water.

NON-SLIP CONCRETE STEPS. Paint with clear paving paint, then sprinkle on some fine sand before the paint dries. When dry, brush off excess sand.

TALCUM POWDER sprinkled in between floor boards stops floors creaking.

USE OLD OIL FROM THE CAR to paint wooden stakes for the garden. Just as good as creosote, and a lot cheaper.

WIPE CAR TYRE WALLS with equal parts glycerine and water after washing and allowing to dry. Adds shine and helps preserve rubber.

WROUGHT-IRON FURNITURE regains its lustre if sponged with a mixture of 1 tablespoon baking soda in 1 litre of water.

CHAPTER SEVEN

MAKING A MEAL OUT OF IT

FOOD TRICKS

ACCOMPANIMENT FOR WAFFLES OR PANCAKES.
Mix together 2 tablespoons honey, 1 tablespoon lemon juice, 1 tablespoon desiccated coconut and 1 teaspoon butter. Heat mixture and spoon over the pancakes while hot.

ADD A LITTLE FINELY CHOPPED APPLE to meat when making sausage rolls.

WHEN PEELING APPLES FOR PRESERVING put them in a large bowl to which two tablespoons of common salt have been added. This not only stops them going brown but keeps them white when cooking.

TO LIVEN UP STEWED APPLE add any of the following: three or four passionfruit; crushed pineapple; guava juice or juice from the skins and cores of quinces.

APPLE PIE WITH A DIFFERENCE. Add a little marmalade and chopped ginger to fruit before baking.

WHEN COOKING APPLES place several passionfruit shells in the saucepan. The pink juice, if left to cool, forms a jelly and gives an unusual flavour.

QUICK APPLE AND BLACKBERRY PIE FILLING. Stew apples with a packet of blackberry jelly.

PLACE THE TOPPING MIXTURE for apple shortcake between two pieces of plastic cling wrap and then roll out. Saves it sticking to the rolling pin and breaking into pieces.

APPLE SHORTCAKE will not go soggy if the cake tin lid is left off until cake is cold.

AUSTRIAN DRINK. Put sour milk in the refrigerator until it is ice cold, then whisk in about 1 tablespoon strawberry jam to each glass of sour milk.

BACON STAYS FRESH IN THE FRIDGE for days if you remove it from the plastic pack and wrap in a tea-towel that has been dampened with vinegar. The towel must be absolutely clean and replaced every other day.

SPRINKLE BACON LIGHTLY WITH FLOUR before cooking to prevent it splattering grease or curling up when frying.

FOR A LIGHTER BANANA CAKE OR LOAF substitute two tablespoons of coconut for two tablespoons of the flour.

STORE UNRIPE BANANAS with ripe bananas and these will ripen quickly.

ADD A BANANA TO STUFFING as accompaniment to beef or steak.

BANANA WAFFLES. Add two sliced bananas to unbeaten egg whites and beat until foamy, then add grated rind of 1 lemon. Increase the sugar by adding an extra tablespoon to the waffle batter with the banana mixture.

BASTE DUCK with a mixture of 2 tablespoons clear honey and 1 tablespoon hot water while roasting. The bird will be golden, crisp and delicious.

BEFORE SLICING BANANAS FOR FRUIT SALAD hold them under cold running water for a minute. They will not turn brown.

ADD A PINCH OF BAKING SODA to any boiled syrup to prevent it crystallising.

BEAN SPROUTS keep well in the fridge in a bowl of water containing some sliced lemon. Change water every day.

FRY COOKED BEETROOT as a breakfast side-dish. Dip slices into a batter made with egg and flour. Fry in hot fat, sprinkle with salt, and serve on slices of hot toast.

SERVE PICKLED BEETROOT hot in a sweet and sour sauce using the liquid in which the vegetable has been preserved as the base of the sauce.

RAW BEETROOT USES
- Grate raw, fresh, young beetroot and spread inside a cheese sandwich.
- Grate and mix with one grated carrot, one grated apple and vinaigrette dressing for salad.
- Beat grated raw beetroot into a thick salad dressing. Use as a garnish in salad.

BISCUITS STAY CRISP in a biscuit tin if a little white sugar is sprinkled on bottom of tin.

RUNNY BLACKBERRY JAM is superb as a topping for ice cream sundaes, and pancakes.

BLACKCURRANT JAM is good accompaniment for liver and bacon.

TO MAKE SOFT BREADCRUMBS for use in a recipe, grate frozen bread or bread rolls on a cheese grater.

BREADCRUMB COATING. Dip food in beaten egg to which half a teaspoon of baking powder has been added, then roll in breadcrumbs.

MIX BREADCRUMBS WITH CHOPPED ONION cooked until tender in hot butter, season with pepper and salt and sprinkle on almost all au gratin or spaghetti dishes. Crisp under griller.

WHEN CRUSHING OVEN-DRIED BREAD to make breadcrumbs, put the slices into a sponge roll tin and crush them with a bread-and-butter plate.

BROWN SUGAR is an antidote for salt. If a stew or soup is too salty, add a small teaspoon of brown sugar and the briny taste will disappear.

BRUSH DOUGH WITH SALTED WATER while it is rising (1 teaspoon to 2 tablespoons water) to ensure a crisp crust.

BURNT TOAST.
- Rub burnt slices together to remove burnt crumbs.
- Rub over a fine grater.

ADD JUICE FROM COOKED CARROTS TO GRAVY for a sweet flavour.

TO DECORATE TOP AND SIDES OF AN ICED CAKE, place a needlework transfer over top or side of cake and with a needle prick through the transfer on to the icing. It will then be quite easy to follow the outline of the design on the icing.

ROLLED ICING FOR CAKES 1 egg white, 500g icing sugar, 50g liquid glucose, a little lemon juice for flavouring and colouring. Sift icing sugar into a bowl and add egg white and melted glucose; draw icing sugar into centre until it is a stiff paste. Knead very well and roll out using cornflour or icing sugar to keep it from sticking. Adhere to cake with very thin water icing or egg white. Rub icing until it is smooth with the hands.

WHEN MAKING COCONUT CAKE soak coconut first in ½ cup of milk so that it does not then absorb the moisture from the cake and dry it out, as so often happens.

TO KEEP SMALL CAKES FRESH never remove the paper that the cake is baked in.

TO STOP WHITE ICING PICKING UP COLOUR from a fruit cake, brush cake over first with white of egg.

PLACE CAKE TIN ON A CLOTH soaked in cold water as soon as it is taken from the oven. Leave a few minutes then run a knife around edge of tin. The cake will come out easily when turned upside down on rack.

CARRY TOMATOES TO A PICNIC in an egg carton to avoid squashing.

CATERING FOR LARGE GROUPS. If serving tea or coffee from a counter, place a pile of saucers at either end of the line of cups which have been set out with all the handles facing towards the patrons.

SPRINKLE GRATED CHEESE OVER TOMATO in a sandwich to absorb the moisture. The sandwich can be cut, wrapped and left overnight without the bread becoming soggy.

FREEZE EXTRA CHEESE SAUCE. Make more sauce than needed, freeze rest in separate portions in containers. When needed, reheat, adding a little milk.

CHEESE WAFFLES are made by adding ¾ cup grated tasty cheese to the batter mixture. Season with extra salt, pepper and mustard. Cayenne pepper may also be added.

CHEESED MUSHROOMS. Fill cavities of mushroom caps with small pieces of sharp cheese, dot with butter, and grill slowly until cheese is melted and mushrooms are cooked through. Serve immediately.

CHICKEN SOUP. Boil chicken carcass for 30 minutes, remove from water, separate the small pieces of chicken from bones and throw carcass away. Add vegetables of your choice to the chicken pieces and broth, season and simmer.

WHEN MAKING CLEAR CHICKEN SOUP put vegetables into a pressure-cooker basket for easier straining after cooking.

CHOCOLATE ICING FOR LAMINGTONS. Dissolve 1 teaspoon gelatin in 1 tablespoon hot water and add to the mixture. (One teaspoon of gelatin is enough for a two-cup capacity mixture of icing.) The gelatin gives more body to the icing which will then cling to the sponge without too much being absorbed.

CHOP COOKED CABBAGE OR SILVERBEET IN THE COLANDER with the edge of a saucer rather than a knife. Saucer fits the contour of the colander and does a quicker job.

CHOPPED CARROT TOPS make a tasty substitute for parsley in white sauce.

SOFTEN CHRISTMAS CAKE ICING by putting a piece of sponge cake in the tin for a few days. Later, use sponge for trifle.

CINNAMON
- Add one teaspoon to crushed cereal or biscuit crumbs used in your baking to give a tangy flavour.

- Add a teaspoon to plain pikelets for variety.
- Sprinkle on a cup of cocoa or drinking chocolate.

CITRUS-FLAVOURED COFFEE. Put a slice of lemon or orange in black coffee for a pleasant change.

SALVAGE CITRUS PEEL FROM THE GRATER
- Use a damp pastry brush to retrieve as much of the peel and pith as possible from between grater edges.
- Grate the citrus peel on to a sheet of paper and then rub some of the weighed sugar through the grater. Every last scrap of peel will come away into the sugar, and into the cake.

COFFEE FIGS.
Soak 500g figs in 500ml strong black coffee overnight then cook them in the liquid, drain and place figs in a serving dish. Simmer the coffee another 10 minutes with sugar, cloves and grated orange rind, then strain, add rum if liked, and pour on to the figs.

MIX COLESLAWS AND SALADS by placing chopped vegetables in a large, snaplock freezer bag. Leave a little air in bag, close top and shake.

COMMON CAKE-BAKING PROBLEMS
- Coarse texture: too much baking powder or too much sugar was used; shortening and sugar were not creamed sufficiently; liquid was insufficient; oven not hot enough.
- Moist, sticky surface: too much sugar used, or sugar not creamed in thoroughly.
- Peak or crack on top: Oven too hot; too much flour used.
- Holey texture: insufficient shortening was used in proportion to the ingredients; over-beaten after flour was added.
- Risen unevenly: oven heat was not evenly distributed; cake not placed in centre of oven shelf. Risen then fallen: too much baking powder was used; oven too slow; cake was taken from oven before completely cooked.

CONTINENTAL-STYLE MUSTARD can be made by mixing dried mustard powder with vinegar and a pinch of sugar. Keeps longer than ordinary mixed mustard.

WHEN MAKING CORDIAL boil the sugar and water for 10 minutes and allow to cool before adding flavouring. Prevents sugar sediment from collecting at the bottom of bottles.

TO KEEP WHIPPED CREAM FIRM LONGER add honey instead of sugar when beating.

CRISPY CHICKEN. Rub mayonnaise over chicken before roasting.

NO-MESS CRUMBLE MIXTURE. Stir dry ingredients then add melted butter and mix thoroughly with a fork. Saves messy hands and fingernails.

STORE CRUMBLE MIXTURE IN FREEZER for use when a quick pudding is needed. It needs no thawing.

WHEN MAKING APPLE CRUMBLE, cook the apples in orange juice sweetened with sugar. Sprinkle grated orange peel over the apple before putting on the crumble top. Serve with whipped cream.

CUCUMBER WITH A DIFFERENCE. Slice thickly, coat in batter and deep fry until golden brown.

CUT CRUMBLY CHEESE with a warm knife.

WHEN BAKING CUSTARD place a few marshmallows in the bottom of the dish. They will rise to the top, melt and make a delicious meringue.

WHISK LUMPY CUSTARD with an eggbeater. Do the same with lumpy sauce, gravy or porridge.

QUICK DESSERT. Dissolve a packet of jelly in one cup of hot water then cut up and stir in some ice cream. Sets immediately. This was my father's favourite.

DIP MUSHROOMS IN HOT WATER before cooking to prevent shrinkage.

EVAPORATED MILK is a good substitute for the egg in an egg-and-breadcrumb batter. It is also a good binder in meat loaf.

FLAVOURING TRICKS
- Insert a clove of garlic or a sprig of rosemary near the bone of roast mutton.
- When frying sections of quince, apple-rings or pineapple slices

Eggs

- **BOILED: BOIL** without breaking the shell by pricking the blunt end with a pin before placing in water. WHEN hard-boiling, add a teaspoon of salt to water for easier shelling. SHELL hard-boiled eggs by cracking around the middle with a teaspoon, then insert spoon between the shell and the egg and gently ease around the egg's circumference – first one half, then the other. The shell simply drops away.
- **FRIED: PLACE** eggs in their shells in boiling water for one minute first. Stops them spreading in the frypan.
- **SCRAMBLED: POUR** the mixture on to some melted butter in the frying pan. When it is beginning to heat, slowly mix with a fork until ready. Scrambled eggs go further if the whites are beaten first. NON-STICK scrambled eggs are easy if the cooking's done in a double boiler. The eggs stay moist and delicious.
- **POACHED: ACHIEVE** well-drained poached eggs (and prevent soggy toast), by using a potato masher instead of an egg slice to remove the eggs from a pan of water. SUBSTITUTE for an egg poacher by greasing the required number of preserving-jar

to serve with cutlets, add a little sugar to the fat. This caramelises and browns the fruit.
- Add cooked, stoned prunes to a lamb stew about 10 minutes before serving.
- Add salad dressing to chopped leftover vegetables and use as a sandwich filling.

FRUIT JUICE-FLAVOURED GLACE ICING. Add a rounded tablespoon of mango/orange flavoured instant fruit drink to glace icing ingredients. Excellent on an apricot jam-filled slice.

FOR A CAKE FILLING THAT WILL STAY SOFT, melt 50g butter, add 150g sifted icing sugar and flavouring, then 2 teaspoons hot water. Stir over low heat for 2 minutes.

---

rings and place them in a flat-bottomed pan of salted water. Gently slip an egg into each ring to cook. Ring will keep eggwhite from spreading.
- **EASY EGG SANDWICH FILLING.** Place a bowl over a pot of steaming water and crack the required number of eggs. Add chutney or relish, mayonnaise, seasoning, a knob of butter and dash of milk; stir until set. Very simple and quite tasty.
- **LEFTOVER EGG YOLKS** make excellent sandwich fillings. Poach them lightly in boiling water, add pepper, salt, butter and whatever other seasoning you like, and mash. This spreads easily and the white of egg is never missed.
- **BEATEN EGG WHITES** are stiffer if eggs have been stored at room temperature rather than in the fridge. Beat whites gently at first, increasing pace as their consistency changes to froth and finally to white "snow". If whites are difficult to stiffen, add a pinch of salt or cream of tartar.
- **SEPARATE YOLK AND WHITE OF EGG** by making small holes at each end of shell. Tip the white out from one end, leaving yolk behind. Sticky tape placed over the holes will keep the yolk fresh for several days.

WHEN BUYING FLOUR, sift the new packet straight into the container it is to be stored in. A great time-saver.

GLAZE FOR FRUIT PIES. Dissolve brown sugar in warm milk and brush over pastry before baking.

SOAK FILLETS OF FISH IN ALE or beer for an hour before dipping in batter and frying.

NO-FRY FISH CAKES. Place on a well-greased oven tray and heat through in a 180 degree C oven until bread crumbed coating turns light golden.

WHEN STEAMING FISH place a piece of cheesecloth in the bottom of the pan. The fish can then be lifted out without it falling apart.

WHEN MAKING FISH STOCK WITH BONES do not allow it to boil hard or a bitter flavour will develop.

WHEN BOTTLING FRUIT, fill a few 100g coffee jars, to give to an elderly neighbour. Seals and bands can be bought for jars this size which hold enough for two desserts.

IF STEWING TART FRUIT such as rhubarb, plums and apples, add a raspberry or strawberry jelly to rhubarb and plums and a lemon jelly to apples. Saves sugar and gives fruit an exciting flavour.

STORE PEELED GARLIC CLOVES in oil in a covered jar. The garlic stays fresh and the oil is useful for dressings.

ADD A LITTLE GELATINE TO GRAVIES when making meat pies and they will not leak when used in school lunches.

STORE ROOT GINGER FOR MONTHS by peeling and slicing and placing covered with sherry in a clean, sealed glass jar. Keep in a cool place or in the refrigerator. The small amount of sherry soaked up does no harm to cooking. Eventually, use gingered sherry dregs in a chicken dish.

TO MAKE A BREAKFAST GRAPEFRUIT LESS TART put a pinch of salt on grapefruit and leave in the fridge overnight. No need for sugar!

PLACE GREASED BAKING TINS in the fridge while mixing cakes or sponges. The cooked cakes will slip out very easily without sticking or breaking.

USE GREASEPROOF PAPER to keep stuffing in place in stuffed poultry. When the bird is cooked, pull out the paper. No mess!

IF HANDS ARE STAINED after peeling fruit for preserving, moisten and rub in some citric acid crystals, then wash in clean water.

WHEN REPLACING SUGAR WITH HONEY in a recipe that involves a liquid, use half the amount of liquid stated.

JAM-SWEETENED TEA. A teaspoon of jam in tea, Russian-style, makes an interesting alternative to sugar.

JELLY IN MINUTES. Place contents of a packet of jelly crystals in a bowl with one cup of boiling water. Stir till dissolved, then add two cups of broken ice. Will set almost immediately while stirring.

LEAVE BREAD TO RISE in a closed car parked outside. Dough warms up even on a cloudy day.

LEFTOVER GINGERBREAD. Slice, steam and serve with custard for a delicious pudding.

LEMON AND HONEY DRINK. For a non-acid drink, use one heaped teaspoon of honey for each glass and dissolve in warm (not hot) water. Add lemon juice and some of the pulp from half a lemon for each glass. Divide evenly into glasses, filling up with cold water, and an ice cube if wished. The dissolved honey can be made in bulk and stored in a screw-top jar in the fridge ready to add to lemon juice and water when wanted.

TO KEEP A LETTUCE FRESH, crisp and green, wrap in tin foil and keep in the fridge.

REMOVE A LETTUCE CORE with a plastic knife to to stop edges browning. Never use a steel knife.

LIVER, BACON AND APPLE. Cut out centres of large, tart apples, fill with minced liver and bacon, season with pepper, mustard or curry powder, and bake in a hot oven until brown.

LOW-FAT TOASTED SANDWICHES. Rub a little butter or margarine on the machine instead of buttering the bread slices. Very little butter is needed.

LUMPY POWDERED INGREDIENTS such as cocoa, custard powder, etc can be broken up into a food processor or blender and processed until smooth. Keep in an airtight container in the freezer.

MARROW SUGGESTION. Cut marrow into serving pieces, lightly spread with ground ginger, sprinkle with salt, pepper and sugar, lay a thin slice of onion and tomato on top and bake around a roast joint, basting frequently.

MASH WATERY POTATOES with milk powder.

FOR DELICIOUS MEATBALLS include crushed root ginger along with garlic. Peel root ginger (a piece the size of a large garlic clove) and use garlic press.

MELT CHOCOLATE in a mixing bowl over a pan of hot water.

MERINGUE TIP. For successful meringues add a pinch of cream of tartar to the beaten meringue mixture.

WHEN MAKING MERINGUES heat the beater beforehand and stand the bowl containing the egg whites in another bowl of hot water while beating. The whites then beat into a froth more quickly.

KEEP MILO IN FRIDGE to prevent it going hard. Store in an airtight container or screw-top jar.

STOP MILK BOILING OVER by placing a pie funnel in saucepan when boiling liquid.

WHEN BOILING MILK or making rice or sago pudding, smear butter on the rim of the pot and the contents will not boil over.

FREEZE MINCE in flat patties for quick thawing.

ADD INTEREST TO MINCE when making rissoles or meat balls with any of the following: chopped celery or onion; cold mashed pumpkin, potato or kumara; cold boiled rice; tomato relish or sauce; worcester sauce; any mixed vegetables.

MINT SAUCE
- De-stalk and wash mint leaves in running water. Place in the blender with the juice of a lemon, the same quantity of hot water and a few tbsps of sugar
- Place washed mint leaves on a chopping board and spoon over 2 tablespoons of raw or demerara sugar. Chop mint finely through sugar, using a chopper or sharp knife. (Sugar will draw out the mint juice and dissolve.) Scrape chopped mint and sugar solution into jug and add malt vinegar to taste.

ADD MINT TO POTATOES five minutes before they are cooked. They keep their flavour better.

MINT AND LEMON CORNED BEEF. To absorb excess grease when cooking corned beef, place a sprig of mint and half a lemon in the cooking water.

MIS-SHAPEN HOME-MADE BRANDY SNAPS can be crumbled and sprinkled over desserts such as apple pie and cream.

QUICK MOUSSE FOR A CHILDREN'S PARTY. Add a medium-sized tin of evaporated milk to a nearly set red jelly, whip through until the mixture has doubled in bulk and is stiff. Add a small bag of chopped jelly beans and whip these through. Serve chilled in tall glasses. Children love it.

FRY AND FREEZE MUSHROOMS when they are plentiful. They can be thawed later and added to soup, pizzas, sauces or casseroles.

NUTS FOR CAKE DECORATIONS should be dipped in milk before baking for a crisp finish.

HEAT NUTS IN SHELLS IN OVEN for a few minutes before trying to crack them.

WHEN BOILING ONIONS add a small teaspoon of sugar to the water to prevent unpleasant onion odour. The sugar will not alter the flavour in any way.

ONION PEELING WITHOUT TEARS
- Chill onions well in fridge before peeling.
- Run cold water over onions before slicing.

PRICK ONIONS FOR ROASTING in several places before placing in the oven. Stops the insides from popping out during cooking.

TO KEEP PEELED ONIONS INTACT when cooking, make an X with a small, sharp knife at the root end of each onion.

OPENING MACADAMIA NUTS
- Heat them in a moderately hot oven before using a nut-cracker.
- Put nuts in the freezer overnight. Shells will be brittle enough to crack easily. After removing nuts from freezer, put them in a mesh bag, and hammer on a solid surface. The mesh bag confines the shell and pieces within, and is far preferable to picking up pieces that have flown in all directions.

BEFORE GRATING ORANGE OR LEMON RINDS dip the grater in cold water. The gratings will then slide off easily and not stick to the grater.

FREEZE ORANGE SEGMENTS for use in fruit drinks and cocktails.

ORANGE GARNISH FOR ROAST LAMB or grilled lamb chops. Dot the orange slices with butter or margarine, sprinkle sparingly with brown sugar and dust lightly with curry powder before grilling.

WHEN COOKING AN ORANGE CAKE add the grated rind to the creamed butter and sugar, then add rest of ingredients. This method flavours the cake better than when the rind is added last.

OVER-COOKED FRUIT CAKE. Fold a thick towel and place over cake while it is cooling.

OVERSPICED STEW OR CURRY. Add plain yoghurt or marmalade to mellow the spicy taste. The marmalade flavour is not evident.

FREEZE PARSLEY in a fairly tight ball in a plastic bag, after removing stalks. When needed, just scrape the side of ball with a knife. Easier than chopping fresh parsley and it keeps well.

DRIED PARSLEY. Wash freshly picked parsley in cold water, then dip in boiling water for 20 to 30 seconds. Spread on brown paper and dry slowly in an oven that is still warm after baking. When dry, crush and take stalks out. Bottle and store. Excellent for use in soups and stews in winter.

QUICK-DRY PARSLEY. Cut up finely, place between paper towels and microwave on high for three minutes. Store in a screw-top jar.

COOK PARSNIPS AND CARROTS together, strain, add a knob of butter and seasoning, and a good sprinkling of finely-chopped parsley.

PARTY JELLY FOR CHILDREN looks and tastes good with a pink frill of apple froth. After cooking stewed apples, add the white of an egg and a drop of cochineal and beat till fluffy. Decorate jelly with this.

COOK PASTA IN A WIRE BASKET in a saucepan. Easy to remove and drain when cooked.

TO STOP PASTA STICKING TOGETHER, and prevent water boiling over, add 1 tablespoon of cooking oil to the water.

PASTRY TIPS
- Flour should always be sieved to let the air through it.
- Weigh all ingredients carefully.
- Mix water into dry ingredients with a metal knife.
- Have pastry just moist enough not to stick to board.
- Keep raw pastry as cool as possible before putting in oven.
- Do not have too much flour on board when rolling pastry.
- Roll out firmly but lightly and handle as little as possible.

IF PAVLOVA STICKS TO TRAY take a piece of strong cotton about 60cm long, hold at both ends and carefully pull under the pavlova.

ALMOND-FLAVOURED PAVLOVA. Add 1 teaspoon almond essence to a pavlova mixture.

PEANUT BUTTER RECIPE. 1kg peanuts (shelled, roasted and peeled), 1 teapoon salt (or to taste), 2-4 tablespoons olive oil, to taste. Blend in food processor for texture required.

FILL A PEPPER POT with white pepper by pouring the pepper powder into an envelope and cutting a small hole in one corner. Saves spills and much sneezing.

TO REHEAT A PIE IN A CONVENTIONAL OVEN take a sheet of greaseproof paper and dip it in cold water. Drip off surplus water, then wrap the pie in the paper, parcel fashion. Heat in a moderate oven. This prevents pastry from becoming hard and dry.

WHEN COOKING A FROZEN PIE put strips of foil around the edge till the middle of the pie is beginning to brown, then remove strips. This eliminates hard, overcooked edges.

WHEN BAKING A PIE put it in an oven roasting bag or a plain paper bag, seal and cut four or five slits in the paper. Place on a biscuit tray and bake 10 minutes longer than the usual time. Crust will turn a beautiful golden brown and oven spills are eliminated.

PIKELET PREPARATION. Rub pan with a cut potato instead of butter for an even browning and more professional result.

USES FOR FRESH PINEAPPLE JUICE
- Add to fruit-flavoured sachet drinks for a fresh-tasting drink.
- Add to soups, stews and casseroles for a pineapple flavour.
- Add to milkshakes for a refreshing change.
- Use instead of water when cooking rhubarb.
- For a sweet pungent sauce for meat dishes, mix cornflour in a little juice, add remaining juice, 1 teaspoon soy sauce and 1 teaspoon vinegar.
- Combine with equal parts of orange juice.

- For a pineapple caramel syrup to pour over ice cream, steamed puddings, etc combine and bring to boil the pineapple juice, ½ cup brown or raw sugar and one tablespoons lemon juice.

PINEAPPLE CIDER. Use one whole pineapple or the skins of four. Put through a mincer and pour on 3 litres of water and leave till next day. Strain. Add four cups of sugar and stir till the sugar is dissolved, then bottle. Ready for drinking after two days.

PIPING BAG. When icing a cake, use a plastic freezer bag with corner cut off. Strong and flexible.

PLACE A WET TOWEL UNDER A MIXING BOWL to keep it from slipping on benchtop.

PORK CHOP COATING. Rub the surface of pork chops with equal parts castor sugar and dry mustard (about 1 teaspoon of each is sufficient for four chops). Delicious.

Lemons

- **FREEZE LEMON JUICE** in ice cubes for later use in drinks and baking.
- **RUB HANDS WITH LEMON JUICE** to remove odours such as garlic and onions.
- **PUT LEMONS DOWN THE WASTE** disposal unit to remove odours.
- **RUB LEMONS OVER RUST** stains to remove.
- **KEEP LEMONS LONGER** by placing them under a glass tumbler.
- **ADD A SMALL PIECE** of lemon to tripe to reduce the smell and make it beautifully tender.
- **REDUCE SMELLS OF CABBAGE,** cauliflower and brussels sprouts by adding a slice of lemon to the cooking water.
- **WHITEN DISCOLOURED CAULIFLOWER** by adding 1 tablespoon lemon juice to cooking water.

FOR CRISP PORK CRACKLING slip a knife under the skin of a pork roast and carefully remove. Two minutes on a separate tray in the oven will crisp it up well.

POTATO SUGGESTIONS.
- When boiling old potatoes, add a squeeze of lemon juice or vinegar to water to whiten. Add a pinch of sugar to make potatoes floury.
- Bake potato peelings in a little oil in a hot oven until crisp.
- Mash finely cut lettuce and boiled potatoes together. Add vinegar or lemon juice to taste and serve with fried bacon or add bacon fat when mashing and serve with chops.
- To make crisp roast potatoes, boil peeled potatoes for five minutes, drain and coat with a little milk. Roast as usual.

TO FREEZE POTATOES SUCCESSFULLY bake firm clean potatoes in skins until just cooked. Wrap each in plastic cling film and bag then freeze. To use, unwrap and heat in a hot oven for 20 minutes.

- **IMPROVE SILVERBEET FLAVOUR** by adding a little lemon juice before serving.
- **LEMONS YIELD MORE JUICE** if they are
  Warmed under the hot tap.
  Placed for a couple of minutes in a warm oven.
  Placed in the microwave for a second or two.
  Rolled hard on a board before cutting and squeezing.
- **TO PRESERVE LEMONS:** Cover with melted paraffin or preserving wax. Simple and very effective.
  Rub lemons all over with petroleum jelly. If they are well cleaned before use, the rind as well as the juice can be used in cooking.
  Put a layer of sand in a box and lay clean lemons in rows, not touching each other. Cover with sand, and continue till box is full. Store in a cool place.

WHEN STUFFING POULTRY mix 1 teaspoon desiccated coconut with the breadcrumbs. Keeps the bird moist.

PRUNE PULP. To make three cups of pulp, cook and stone 500g prunes.

FOR A QUICK SNACK fry a small sliced onion and two rashers of finely chopped bacon in a tablespoon of butter till tender. Add a tin of sweetcorn and a cup of white sauce. Serve hot on buttered toast garnished with parsley.

A QUICK SWEET: fill a flan case with grated apple and top with 3 tablespoons condensed milk and 3 tablespoons of coconut. Bake in a slow oven until golden brown.

QUICK AND EASY WHITE SAUCE. Beat together equal quantities of flour and butter and chill. Cut into squares and freeze. Depending on the thickness of the sauce, drop one or two squares into one cup of milk and heat, stirring while it thickens.

ADD HONEY TO RHUBARB instead of sugar when cooking to make rhubarb less tart.

RECYCLE FOIL COFFEE REFILL PACKS. Cut off the tops and bases, split the seams and use the foil to line cake tins. Wash and wipe before use.

RED-COLOURED jelly crystals added to hot stewed rhubarb give colour and substance. Dessert may be eaten hot or left to set and served cold with cream or ice-cream.

REMOVE FAT FROM STEWS AND SOUPS by drawing a piece of clean paper towel across surface before serving.

STEAMED RICE ON AN ELECTRIC STOVE TOP. Pour rice into a small saucepan to reach almost to the first joint of your finger.

Add enough cold water to reach the second joint (about twice as much water as rice). Put tight-fitting lid on pan, turn heat to high and bring water to boil. Turn heat off immediately and leave rice to cook for 10 minutes in the steam. Do not remove lid. When cooked, rice comes away easily from pan. Serves four.

ADD A THIMBLEFUL OF RICE to a salt shaker to keep salt dry and free-flowing.

NON-STICK RICE.
Add a knob of butter to the boiling water before adding the rice. The grains will stay separate. A squeeze of lemon juice will keep the rice white.

RIPEN FRUIT QUICKLY by placing in a plastic bag with a ripe apple and tie the top of the bag. Check the fruit daily. Very good for kiwifruit, persimmons and feijoas.

RIPEN NASHI PEARS by leaving in a paper bag with some apples for two days.

ROAST A LOIN OF PORK with prunes and apples and avoid the need to make apple sauce. The quantity of prunes and apples will depend on the size of the roast. Peel and slice apples and stone the prunes. With a sharp knife, partially remove meat from the bone and stuff an equal quantity of apple and prunes down between the meat and the bone. Tie meat back on the bone and roast in the usual way.

RUN COLD WATER IN THE SINK while pouring hot water from a pan of vegetables to prevent steam scalding hands.

RUN COLD WATER OVER A GRATER before using it on butter. Stops the butter congealing.

FOR A DIFFERENT SANDWICH FILLING try cold, cooked broccoli with a sprinkling of salt. It is similar to asparagus and quite delicious.

USE A SANDWICH-MAKER to toast peanuts in.

MIX SALT AND PEPPER TOGETHER in one big container for use in the kitchen or on a picnic.

BEFORE COOKING SAUSAGES put them unseparated into a saucepan and boil them for a little while. This prevents them coming out at both ends when you fry them.

NO-FUSS SAUTE. Chop bulk quantities of garlic, ginger and onion in a food processor, mix with oil and freeze in ice-cube trays.

SAVOURY BREAD PUDDING. Start as if making sweet bread pudding but use no sugar. Add pepper and salt and chopped bacon and parsley. Sprinkle top with grated cheese. Cook in moderate oven for 30 minutes.

SAVOURY PIKELETS. Make an ordinary pikelet mixture, leaving out the sugar. Then mince 250g beefsteak, 125g tomatoes, 1 bacon rasher, a little parsley. Add to the mixture. Cook on a medium to hot element.

FRESHEN UP LEFTOVER SCONES by placing them in a covered saucepan over a low heat for about five minutes. Turn off the heat and leave the saucepan on the element for another five minutes. The warmth in the enclosed pan produces "fresh" scones.

HOLD SILVERBEET UP TO LIGHT when washing it, to check for dirt and bugs.

SHORTBREAD SLICES
Instead of rolling and cutting shortbread into shapes, form it into a roll and slice to the required thickness.

SHORTCAKE FILLING ½ tin condensed milk, 2 tablespoons golden syrup, 50g melted butter, 2 tablespoons sugar, vanilla to taste, a little lemon juice. Mix all together and put between layers of shortcake and bake 1 hour in a slow oven.

KEEP SCONES FRESH by adding a teaspoon of golden syrup to scone mixture. Dissolve in the liquid with the salt before adding to the flour. Use 1 dessertspoon of cornflour to every 500g flour to improve texture.

SLICING A MEAT LOAF is easier if loaf is left in its pan for ten minutes after cooking.

SOFT BROWN SUGAR creams better than castor sugar with butter and saves time when baking.

SOFTEN BUTTER FOR SPREADING by placing in a bowl in the hotwater cupboard.

LEFTOVER SOUR CREAM
- Use to baste a meat loaf or oven-baked fish fillets.
- Put it into mayonnaise.
- Add some to scone mixture.
- Add to a cheese or parsley sauce.
- Blend into creamy mashed potato.
- Use as a dressing for shredded carrot, lettuce, celery and cabbage.
- Add to chilled beetroot, cucumber or avocado soup. Make sure the cream is quite sour. To speed the souring process, if necessary, add a little lemon juice.

WHEN COOKING WITH SOUR CREAM never allow it to boil or it may curdle. Heat the cream separately very gently, then add to dish.

RULES FOR SPICED FRUITS
- Always choose fresh, good quality fruit free from blemishes,

and uniform in size. Imperfect, irregular fruits may be cut up and used in relishes.
- Fruits may be slightly under-ripe but never over-ripe.
- All fruit should be washed gently but thoroughly to remove dirt and grit.
- Use a top quality, full-strength vinegar. Weak vinegar does not preserve fruit adequately and may result in spoilage. Too strong a vinegar can cause fruit to shrivel. Distilled white vinegar is the most neutral flavoured vinegar.
- The selection of spices is important. Fresh, whole spices should be used unless the recipe specifically calls for them to be ground. Spices which are not fresh may give a "dusty" or off flavour to your pickled fruit.

WHEN WASHING STRAWBERRIES do so before removing the stalks. Otherwise the fruit will becoming soggy.

LEFTOVER STUFFING from chicken or meat can be rolled into balls and quickly browned in butter or cooked around the meat.

SPOON MINT JELLY INTO PEAR HALVES and serve with roast lamb.

SPRING ONIONS from the supermarket will grow in the garden if you rest them overnight in water, then plant out.

SPRINKLE PEPPER OVER CUT SURFACES OF PUMPKIN if storing. Pumpkin will stay fresh, even without refrigeration.

STEW APPLES AND TAMARILLOS together, then bottle them. The apples absorb the rich red colour and the tamarillos are not so strongly flavoured.

STORING SMALL CAKES IN A TIN. To prevent them being squashed, put a cup in the middle of the tin and place the cakes around it. Put a plate on top of the cup and place second layer on this.

STORE LEMONS IN WITH BAKING SUGAR for a hint of lemon flavour in baking.

STORE RECIPES FROM MAGAZINES or given by friends in flipover plastic photo albums. Easy to see and always clean.

STORE WHOLEMEAL FLOUR AND WHOLE GRAINS in airtight containers in the fridge.

SUBSTITUTE FOR HORSERADISH SAUCE. Use white turnip, scraped and mixed with a little mustard, vinegar and milk.

SWEET PASTRY GLAZE. Mix a little brown sugar into milk and brush over raw pastry before baking.

THICKEN STEWS AND CASSEROLES with mashed potato rather than flour for a smoother gravy. Or grate a potato finely into the hot fluid and cook for a further five to ten minutes.

TENDER CORNED BEEF. Add 1 tablespoon golden syrup and 1 tablespoon vinegar to corned beef, bring to boil quickly, and then gently simmer for a long time.

TENDERISE MEAT by rubbing well before cooking with a mixture of vinegar and golden syrup in the proportion of two teaspoons of vinegar to one-and-a-half teaspoons of syrup. Leave for two hours. The result is excellent. The meat is tender and cooks faster, and the mixture leaves no taste.

TEST WAFFLE IRON FOR CORRECT HEAT by dropping ½ teaspoon water on it. If the water boils in small balls, the waffle iron is ready to use. If it sizzles away quickly it is too hot; if it just runs it is not hot enough.

TART RHUBARB. Cover chopped stalks with boiling water and leave to steep. Strain and cook as normal. Tartness disappears.

THICKEN VEGETABLE SOUPS with one or two cups of grated pumpkin.

TO PREPARE UNCOOKED MEAT PATTIES for freezing, spoon the mixture into paper patty cases. Stack them on top of one another and squash down. This way they can be separated when still frozen.

TOAST COARSELY GRAINED BREAD in oven till golden, serve with warm milk and honey as a change from breakfast cereal.

TOMATO SAUCE THAT WON'T POUR. Push a drinking straw to the bottom of the bottle, remove straw and sauce will flow freely.

FREEZE WHOLE TOMATOES before they get too ripe. They stay firmer this way when defrosted and can be cut to required size.

TOMATOES PEEL EASILY if frozen then rinsed under the hot tap.

USE A SMALL SAUCEPAN AS A SCOOP when removing fruit, etc from a preserving pan to pour into jars. Handle stays clean and the saucepan will hold a larger quantity than a cup. Make sure pan has a lip.

USES FOR ALUMINIUM FOIL
- Turn an open ovenware dish into a casserole by moulding a piece of foil over the top.
- When reheating a portion of pie, prevent pastry from drying out by moulding a piece of foil over the dish.
- Use to line baking dishes, cake tins, grill pan, etc to eliminate a large and messy wash-up.
- Mould a piece of foil to bowl underneath an electric stovetop element. Reflects heat and catches spills.

FRESHEN LIMP VEGETABLES
- Cauliflower, cabbage, celery and silverbeet. Remove at least

half the limp leaves, cut a paper-thin slice off the bottom of the core or stalk to get rid of any dirt. Put 5mm cold water into a pot, add vegetables and stand in fridge for about two hours. Keep vegetables fresh for a week if a thin slice is shaved from the core and the water changed daily.
- Lettuce. Plunge whole lettuce (core removed) into iced water. Add a teaspoon of sugar, and weight the lettuce down so it is completely submerged. Leave for an hour, then wash the crisp leaves as usual.
- Carrots. Stand in a mixture of very cold water and sugar for 30 minutes before using.
- Celery. Stand in a jug of cold water with one teaspoon of salt added for a few hours.

STORE SHELLED WALNUTS in a container in the freezer to keep them fresh for months.

WARM NUTS AND FRUIT BEFORE COATING with flour and adding to a cake and they will never sink.

YORKSHIRE PUDDING success depends on the temperature of the milk. Use only a small quantity of milk when mixing together the necessary flour, egg and salt. The remainder of the milk should be very hot when added. This does the trick. Use small individual tins and the puddings will puff up and be very light.

YOUNG BROAD BEANS can be cooked in the same way as runner beans.

CHAPTER EIGHT
Anything & Everything

GENERAL HINTS

A SWINGING CUPBOARD DOOR can be fixed by pressing a drawing-pin into the door's lower edge. This will raise door just enough to make contact with the catch.

ANT DETERRENTS
- Plug a cotton wool ball soaked with eucalyptus oil into the place of entry.
- Sprinkle places of entry, shelves, crevices, etc with black pepper, salt, ground cloves or powdered camphor.
- Mix a packet of dry yeast with 1 tablespoon of sugar, place mixture in containers in cupboards and under the house.
- Place cucumber peelings on a saucer on bench when preparing food.
- Commercial sprays are effective. Spray areas of entry.

BEFORE FILLING A HOT-WATER BOTTLE, rinse it out with hot water, lie it flat on benchtop with neck upright and push out any air. Fill carefully. Add salt to hot water to keep it hot for longer.

BLU-TACK IS BETTER THAN TAPE for wrapping gifts. It's reusable and doesn't rip the paper.

BURGLAR-PROOF THE LOO by fixing a small bolt to the outside of the toilet door. When the room is not in use it can be locked from the outside and any intruder who climbs through the louvre window will be foiled.

CATERING-SIZED TEABAG.
To use loose tea in a giant teapot, make a large teabag, 20cm by 18cm, from net. Turn over at the top to make a hem for putting a drawstring through. Empty bag, wash and dry out after use. More cost efficient than using lots of teabags!

CHIPPED CRYSTAL VASE. Sand down rough edges with a fine emery board or sandpaper to make chip almost invisible.

COPY THE ADDRESS to which you are sending a parcel onto a piece of paper and include inside before wrapping it. If the address on the outside becomes illegible for any reason, the post office can get the address from the inside and send it on.

CREATE A NATURAL AIR FRESHENER by leaving dead lavender flowers (stalks removed) in the sun with some rose petals. When dried, mix together and add dried rosemary and essential oil.

CUTTINGS FROM THE NEWSPAPER make interesting reading for a friend overseas.

DIP CANDLE ENDS IN HOT WATER to soften them before fixing in candleholders.

DRIED-OUT BALLPOINT PENS can be revived by running under very hot water.

DROP 10 CENTS INTO A PIGGYBANK BY THE PHONE each time you make a call. Money for the phone bill will mount up.

DRY OFF WASHED PLASTIC BAGS by pegging them on a wire coat hanger and hanging in the hot water cupboard for a couple of days.

DUST INSIDES OF RUBBER GLOVES with talcum powder before use for easy removal later.

FLIES WILL STAY OFF WINDOWS AND MIRRORS if glass is rubbed with vinegar on a clean cloth.

FLY REPELLENT
- Heat lavender oil in an aromatherapy burner .
- Keep basil and mint plants in pots on kitchen window-sill.

FLY SPECKS ON BOOKS rub away with a soft eraser. Or you can use soft, very fresh bread. Work bread with fingers into a small ball that will roll over the paper until clean. For heavy art paper, scrape gently with a knife to lift speck.

FOR A FRAGRANT LINEN CUPBOARD store incense on floor.

FREE A ZIP THAT IS STIFF OR STUCK. For metal zip, run a lead pencil along the teeth, or use a cotton bud to dab the zip with a very small amount of CRC (be careful to keep CRC off the material). For a plastic zip, sprinkle with talcum powder to keep it working.

FUSE WIRE should be kept by the fuse box with a small torch nearby for when a fuse blows.

GINGER BEER CORKS WILL NOT POP if they are placed in boiling water for a few minutes before use.

HOME CORRESPONDENT. If you write regular letters to people, keep a note of the date you write and news you relate, to avoid repetition.

KEEP A LARGE BEACH TOWEL IN THE CAR. Use it as a picnic blanket, to kneel on to change a tyre, as a jacket when cold and to put on the lap of a child who may be carsick.

USES FOR OLD KNEEHIGHS AND PANTIHOSE

- Use for straining skin off old paint.
- Hang up and store onions or gladioli corms in them, keeping air circulating.
- Tie plants to stakes with them.
- String pantihose through sleeves of jumpers when drying them on a clothes line, to avoid peg damage.
- Stuff them with rags and use as draught stopper at doors.

HANG BELTS from their buckles on coathooks.

HATS STORED IN SEALED PLASTIC BAGS with a little air in them will not crush.

INDENT MARKS ON A CARPET
- Apply a warm iron over a damp cloth. The carpet pile will lift back up and the marks will disappear.
- Hold a hot steam iron above the carpet marks for a few seconds, then brush lightly. Don't touch carpet fabric with the iron or it may scorch.

JAMMED LOCKS
Rub key in butter, margarine or vaseline and work backwards and forwards in lock to ease it.

MAKE RUN-PROOF LUGGAGE LABELS by allowing writing to dry thoroughly, then rubbing over surface with a slightly warmed candle end.

MEASURE THE SPREAD OF YOUR HAND and you will always have a measuring rule on you.

REPAIR NET CURTAINS with a dab of clear nail polish.

Here's a Hint...

USES FOR OLD SOCKS
- Wear on hands to keep shoe polish off while polishing shoes.
- Put on hands as dusters for fiddly jobs.
- Slip over a broom handle and secure with a rubber band for dusting hard-to-reach corners.
- Keep an old sock handy for when the phone rings and your hands are dirty.

MOHAIR TRAVELLING RUGS are good substitutes for wool underlays on beds.

NAIL SCREWTOP JAR LIDS to underside of shelves in kitchen, workshop or garage. Fill jars with corks, rubber rings, string, nails, screws, etc and screw jars onto the lids.

NOTE DOWN SERIAL NUMBERS of all electrical equipment and items such as bikes and cameras, in case of theft. Keep list separate from the equipment.

OLD TELEPHONE BOOKS are handy for reference when you're out on the road. Keep one in the car.

PAPER RUBBISH BAGS. To maximise space, staple bag closed rather than folding top over. Will also keep neighbourhood dogs out of the rubbish on collection day.

PARTYING ON A WET NIGHT. If you need somewhere to hang guests' wet coats, attach a rod to laundry wall and hang several coathangers on it. Put an old towel on the floor beneath to absorb the drips.

PICNIC TABLECLOTHS won't blow away if you sew pockets at the corners to hold a few small stones as anchors.

PREVENT A GLASS FROM CRACKING when filling with very hot water by standing a metal spoon in the glass.

PUT A DAB OF BLU-TACK or plasticine under small ornaments to hold them firmly on a narrow shelf.

PLACES TO STORE MOTHBALLS
- Put in the fingers of old gloves and hang in wardrobes or on cupboard shelves.
- Punch holes in the lids of small screwtop jars and place mothballs inside for cupboards.

REMOVE A STRONG SMELL FROM A BOTTLE by adding 4 teaspoons dry mustard to some cold water, filling bottle and leaving overnight. Rinse well.

REPLACE A BOTTLE CORK by putting it in boiling water for a short time until it is soft enough to work back into the bottle.

SCRATCHES ON GLASSES. Rub with toothpaste on a soft cloth.

SCRUNCHED-UP NEWSPAPER IN WET SHOES keeps leather supple and prevents shoes drying out of shape.

SHAGPILE CARPET can be groomed with a lightweight bamboo garden rake.

SHAKE AN UMBRELLA BEFORE OPENING to put the ribs in place.

SILK SCARVES won't crease if wrapped around a cardboard roll.

SKIRTS WILL STAY ON A STANDARD COATHANGER without slipping if a rubber band is wound around each end of the coathanger.

SOUVENIR TEATOWELS joined together with a plain cotton backing make a good picnic tablecloth.

SQUEAKY DOOR HINGES will ease up if rubbed with soap.

STORE VALUABLE DOCUMENTS IN FREEZER while on holiday. It is the one place in the house which is fireproof. (Place papers in tightly sealed plastic bag first.)

STOW HEAVY TRUNKS AND PACKING CASES on two sawn-off broom handles placed parallel to wall. Cases will roll out easily when needed.

STRAY CAT IN THE KITCHEN? Don't try to chase it out or it will panic. Instead, walk outside and leave the door wide open. The cat will soon exit, without causing trouble.

STYROFOAM PACKING SHEETS make useful noticeboards.

THROW SCARVES OVER A COATHANGER CROSSBAR to keep them crease-free.

TIGHT-FITTING DRAWERS will slide more easily if the top edges are rubbed with soap or candle wax.

TO FIND A MISSING NEEDLE OR PIN on the carpet, turn lights out and use a torch. In daylight, move a magnet over the area.

TO PREVENT A STATIC SHOCK when getting out of a car, hold on to the metal edge of the car door, then put your feet on the ground. Contact with the ground acts as an earth.

UNTANGLE KNOTS IN SILVER AND GOLD CHAINS by using pins instead of fingers.

USE TWO PICTURE HOOKS, placed a little way apart, to hang a picture. It won't slip askew on the wall.

WATERPROOF A LEAKING VASE by painting inside with varnish.

WHEN A RING IS STUCK on a finger, wash hands in hot water, rub ring finger with soap and work until ring loosens.

WHILE TIDYING THE HOUSE, put small odds and ends of rubbish in a kneehigh stocking for sorting and throwing out later.

WIPE LIGHT BULBS with a tissue sprinkled with perfume to keep rooms smelling fresh.

Living on a budget

BAKING SODA is a cheap deodorant for carpets and upholstery. Sprinkle over, leave for quarter of an hour, then vacuum.

BRIQUETTES FOR A FIRE can be made from torn up old newspapers. Place torn papers in a 4.5 litre container, add enough water to soak and leave until quite soft and pulpy, stirring now and again. To this, add as much coal dust as it will take, and mix in thoroughly. Include a small proportion of sawdust too, if available. Take handfuls of the mixture and press into egg shapes, squeezing out any excess water. Place briquettes out to dry on a length of corrugated iron or a flat board. Leave for about a month, then put in bag or bin and use.

CANDLES BURN MORE SLOWLY if kept in freezer until needed.

CHECK HOT WATER THERMOSTAT to ensure it is not set too high (ACC recommends 55 deg C).

COOK STEWS AND CASSEROLES ON STOVETOP rather than in the oven to save on power.

CUT UP OLD TABLECLOTHS for use as tea towels.

ECONOMICAL ALL-PURPOSE CLEANER. Put 1 tablespoon each of

methylated spirits and kerosene in a ½-litre glass bottle. Fill up with water and shake well before applying with a soft damp cloth to windows, chrome and stainless steel sinks and benches. Removes finger marks from painted surfaces and leaves a good shine. Finish off with a dry cloth. Keep lid on bottle.

FILL A LARGE THERMOS WITH BOILING WATER to save you boiling the jug each time you want a hot drink.

IF ONLY ONE PERSON NEEDS WARMING in a room, use a hot water bottle, rug or eiderdown and wear more clothes. Remember that wool clothing is warmer than synthetics.

LAMP SHADES that direct light efficiently allow the use of lower wattage bulbs.

NEVER FAVOUR ONE STOVETOP ELEMENT more than the others. It will wear out more quickly, and it is not good for the other elements to be left unused.

NEW KNOBS FOR OLD SAUCEPANS. Push a sharp-pointed screw up through the hole. Twist a cork on to it firmly. The cork makes a fine, heat-proof handle at no cost.

PLACE DRAUGHT-SEALERS around badly fitting windows to save on heating.

QUICK FIRELIGHTERS. Soak newspapers in water, roll into balls and dry in the sun.

RECYCLE LABELS from tin cans as scrap paper.

REFLECTORS ON RADIANT HEATERS should be kept clean and dust-free so that they throw out maximum heat.

SAVE CANDLE ENDS to use as fire-lighters.

SHAVING CREAM makes a cheap, effective, upholstery cleaner. Lifts grime and removes stains from most surfaces.

STACK DIRTY DISHES and wash up only once a day.

TURN OFF LIGHTS in rooms not being used.

USE COLD WATER when washing clothes and cleaning hands.

WEAR WARMER CLOTHES when sitting still for long periods, to save on heaters.

WHITE VINEGAR is an efficient and inexpensive all-purpose bathroom cleaner. Good on tiles, floors and porcelain surfaces.

WORN CHILDREN'S BLANKETS. When these are looking thin and worn and losing warmth, cover the thin parts with pastel-coloured flannel patches in the shape of rabbits, cats or ducks. Blanket-stitch them on, and mark eyes with large French knots.

Food on a budget

BAKING IN BULK. To save time and make three different cakes from the same basic ingredients, prepare a double quantity of plain cake mix and divide it into three. Use one third for a plain iced cake, one third for cup cakes and the rest for a marble cake – add a little spice and cocoa to half of the marble cake mixture.

BREADCRUMBS IN MEAT LOAF or mince patties add bulk and stop meat from "caking".

BRUSH PIE CRUSTS WITH MILK AND CUSTARD POWDER as a good substitute for egg.

BULK-BUY COOKING CHEESE and grate it, placing it loosely in lidded plastic containers and storing in freezer. Keeps fresh for weeks and is ready for immediate use.

CHEAP FRUIT YOGHURT can be made by chopping up fresh fruit into natural yoghurt. Peach, kiwifruit, orange and apple pulp add plenty of bulk.

LEMON JUICE ECONOMY. Prick lemon with a pin, satay stick or skewer to squeeze out juice as needed. Store lemon in fridge, wrapped in foil.

MAKE USE OF WARM OVEN AFTER BAKING by putting pieces of bread on an oven tray and covering with vegemite. Cut into finger pieces and heat in oven until golden brown. Let cool, then place in an air-tight container. Excellent for parties and snacks.

MINCE GOES FURTHER if some crushed Weetbix is added to the mixture.

MIX LEFTOVER MASHED POTATO with 1 egg, 1 tablespoon flour, a small grated onion and some chopped parsley. Fry tablespoon amounts in oil or butter until golden each side.

OUTER LEAVES OF LETTUCE can be turned into soup.

PART-COOK ROASTING VEGETABLES IN MICROWAVE before adding to meat. Quicker than part-cooking on the stovetop, and saves power.

SAUSAGES ARE ECONOMICAL and more sustaining when casseroled because they absorb liquid, making them filling. Cook your favourite recipe in a casserole dish on the stovetop.

SERVE LEFTOVER LAMB cut up into slices; dip it in tomato sauce, roll in breadcrumbs and fry in oil until golden brown.

STORE UP FOR CHRISTMAS by buying one extra tinned item each week for a few months beforehand. Keep at the back of your storecupboard until needed.

TENDER BEEF CASSEROLE FROM A CHEAP CUT. Freeze then slice the meat very thinly with a sharp knife. Put the thin slices into casserole with onion, flavourings, stock or water and cook slowly, for longer than usual, with a lid on or a foil plate over the top.

The next generation

APPLY BARRIER CREAM to young rugby players' knees (it does not show). Mud and grass stains soak off easily in the shower.

BATHING A VERY YOUNG BABY. Keep a firm hold by wearing a cotton glove on the hand used to support the baby.

BLEACH NAPPIES by soaking in water with a teaspoon of peroxide added, then hanging out to dry in strong sunshine.

CHILDREN'S SHOE LACES. Before threading all the way to top of shoe, tie a knot in laces on either side of second hole. Laces will stay in place.

DECORATE A CHILD'S PLASTER CAST by sticking animal or flower transfers on to the white plaster.

HANG MODEL AIRCRAFT on some fishing line and pin to a child's bedroom ceiling.

INVITATIONS FOR A CHILDREN'S PARTY. Write on fallen leaves with felt pen.

KEEP TODDLERS OCCUPIED when you're busy in the kitchen by putting old saucepans, lids and plastic mixing bowls in a low drawer that the child can open unaided.

MAKE A SHADY PLAY AREA by hanging a large sheet over a clothesline.

MARK CHILDREN'S PLASTIC SANDALS with a dab of paint on the inner sole – a different colour for each child.

NO-MESS PAINTING. Fill an empty deodorant bottle with non-toxic paint – the roller ball runs easily across paper and is easy for a child to use.

PROTECT CHILDREN'S BUS PASSES by covering with clear, self-adhesive vinyl.

REMOVE CHEWING GUM FROM CHILDREN'S HAIR with peanut butter.

STACKABLE PLASTIC VEGETABLE RACKS are good as storage for children's toys.

TEACH A PRE-SCHOOLER ABOUT COLOURS with a colour chart from a local paint shop. They will learn to distinguish degrees of light and dark as well as the basic colour differences.

TEMPORARY SANDPIT. Turn a paddling pool into a sandpit in winter by filling with clean white sand.

TO STOP SMALL CHILDREN ROLLING OUT OF BED
- Put top sheet lengthwise across the bed and tuck in firmly.
- Sew a length of flannelette to edges of a blanket, where it is to be tucked in.

USE A HAND TOWEL INSTEAD OF A BIB to keep a toddler's clothes clean at mealtimes. Sew tapes to two corners and tie.

TRIM TOPS OFF PLASTIC DRINK BOTTLES with a sharp knife. Use the see-through bases to hold children's playthings such as marbles, or matchbox cars.

WAX AND CHALK CRAYONS will last longer if clear adhesive tape is wrapped around each crayon. Tape can be gradually peeled off as crayon wears down.

WOODEN SWING.
Stick a piece of rubber on seat for a non-slip surface, and to prevent splinters.

Looking after yourself

AN EMPTY HAND CREAM TUBE can be cut in half with scissors – surprise yourself at the amount still remaining in both sections. Cover the cut ends with cling film.

ARTHRITIS PAIN
- Place one teaspoonful of honey, one teaspoonful of cider vinegar in a glass and add boiling water. Take each morning. This is a common American folk cure, with numerous testimonials to its virtue.
- Put one and a half cups of whisky and one packet of chillies in a jar, seal for 48 hours, then strain and throw away the chillies. Put three drops of the mixture in your first cup of tea each day. Capsicum tincture, made in much this way, was a common folk remedy for sore joints even as recently as 50 years ago. Brandy or vodka can be used as well as whisky. The tincture can be painted on the sore joint, too.

AVOID DAMAGE TO METAL EARRINGS if using hairspray by putting on jewellery after spraying, not before.

BAKING SODA is ideal for healing small mouth ulcers. Place a small amount on affected area.

CLEAN SPECTACLES by putting a drop of vinegar on each lens and polishing with a soft duster or cloth.

COLDS
- Mix one tablespoonful of honey in a glass with one teaspoonful of salt. Put a little on a spoon, let it dissolve in the mouth and swallow slowly. The honey is soothing and the salt cuts the phlegm. It is helpful with bronchitis or cold on the chest.
- Cut pieces of garlic clove into a cupful of two tablespoonfuls of vinegar and two tablespoonfuls of demerara sugar mixed. Let stand for about 10 minutes. Take one or two teaspoonfuls to begin with, then one teaspoonful every four hours. Brown sugar may be substituted and the garlic pieces can be removed after a while. It works well for bronchitis, too.

TO RELIEVE COUGH OR SORE THROAT, slice an onion, cover with sugar, preferably brown, and take a few sips of the syrup that forms. There are several chemicals of proven medicinal value in onion or garlic. Even the inhaled vapour of an onion may do good. Deodorised extracts of garlic from health food stockists are now popular.

CRAMP IN LEGS AND FEET
- At night, wrap a handful of small corks in large handkerchief and place in bottom of bed, or put camphor blocks between the sheets.
- Place a cold, wet cloth around the painful parts.
- Apply ice or a frozen pack.
- Increased calcium in the diet may ease cramps.

CRACKED HEELS
- Rub with a loofah or nail brush to keep the skin soft. After every wash massage in some vitamin E cream.
- Rub with olive oil night and morning. The skin soon becomes soft and smooth.

> **Here's a Hint...** TO CURE HICCUPS, take one teaspoon of vinegar at intervals. It is not an unpleasant taste, as most of us like pickled onions and beetroot. A friend of mine had a bad hiccup attack for four days and tried the vinegar remedy in desperation – she was cured. – B B, Whangarei

- Soften and remove flaky skin with a mud pack.

EFFECTIVE HAIR BRUSHING
Brush upwards from base of neck to crown, from temples to crown, and from forehead to crown. This stimulates the scalp and improves hair texture.

FOR ITCHY INSECT BITES, dissolve one teaspoon of baking soda in two teaspoons of water and dab on the affected areas.

FRESH HERBS tied in a bunch and suspended from the bath tap make a delightful herbal bath.

GARLIC BREATH can be countered by chewing fresh parsley, mint, celery or a coffee bean.

HAIR CONDITIONER
Whip together the yolks of three eggs with a few drops of apple cider vinegar, a few drops of glycerine and wheatgerm or almond oil. For best results warm the oil gently before adding other ingredients. Massage through hair and leave for at least 30 minutes before washing it.

HOME-MADE SCENTED SACHET. Spray cottonwool balls with a favourite perfume and slip into squares of cotton material, sewn together on three sides. Gather the fourth side, pull up gathers and attach bow or ribbon. Keeps underwear drawer smelling pretty.

LOOSEN TOPS OF NAIL POLISH BOTTLES when stuck by running top of bottle under warm water for a few moments.

MASCARA REMAINS can be used up on eyebrows. If applied lightly, consistency is just right to make ageing eyebrows look natural.

MASSAGE SCAR TISSUE with a capsule of vitamin E oil or peanut oil.

NAIL POLISH will last longer if the nails are wiped with vinegar before applying.

OATMEAL REMEDIES
- For a reviving facial, combine enough fine oatmeal and cold cream to cover face, avoiding sensitive areas around the eyes. Massage into the skin for three or four minutes before rinsing off.
- To soften rough hands, sprinkle oatmeal on palms and rub together for a few moments.

OILY HAIR. Add a few drops of vinegar or lemon juice to the water when rinsing your hair. Massage your scalp gently but firmly.

PROTECT LUXURY PANTIHOSE by washing before wearing, then spraying with an unperfumed hairspray.

PUT EYE PENCILS AND LIPLINERS IN FREEZER for 10 to 15 minutes before sharpening.

REMOVE TAR FROM HANDS or feet with olive oil.

SOFTEN AND WHITEN HANDS AFTER GARDENING by putting a teaspoon of sugar into the palm of your hand, adding about two teaspoonfuls of lemon juice and working the sticky mess into your hands for as long as you can spare. Rinse off.

SPRINKLE SALT over dry hair for the easiest dandruff treatment ever. Massage it into the scalp well, then shampoo thoroughly.

SOAK HAIR BRUSHES AND COMBS in a mixture of 1 dessertspoon baking soda and 2 cups boiling water to clean.

STOP A LADDER IN PANTIHOSE FROM RUNNING by applying hairspray. Does not leave a mark as nail-polish tends to do.

STORE NAIL VARNISH IN THE FRIDGE to stop it sticking.

STY ON EYELID
- Rub the affected area gently with a piece of gold jewellery – for instance a wedding ring. Then bathe eye in cold water.
- A teabag still warm from the cup applied to the sty is a common home remedy.

SUNBURN RELIEF. Soak in a bath of lukewarm water to which a tablespoon of baking soda has been added.

TEMPORARY RELIEF FROM TOOTHACHE. Add two drops of clove oil to a cup of hot water and rinse mouth out. Good as a gargle for sore throats.

TIME OUT IN THE GARDEN. Five minutes or so spent in the garden is an amazing reviver on a tough day, even if you just step out for a look.

TIRED FEET. Wash and dry feet then dab on methylated spirits with cotton wool.

TO REMOVE A PLASTER FROM SENSITIVE SKIN rub baby oil over until quite moist.

USE A POT-PLANT SPRAYER with water to dampen your hair in the morning when it looks slept-on.

WARTS

- Rub the inside of a banana skin on to warts.
- Apply the liquid from the stem of a dandelion flower.
- Dab on a solution of washing soda and water.
- Cut a slice from a potato from just near the skin and rub it on warts night and morning.
- Rub castor oil on the warts regularly.

INDEX

A

acrylic bath cleaning 29
air freshener natural 95
aluminium window frames, cleaning 44
aluminum saucepans 17, 24
animal hairs on carpet, furniture 44
ant deterrents 94
anti-static remedy for synthetics 34
antique brooch 51
aphids 56
apple sauce substitute 87
apple, and blackberry 67, crumble 73, pie 66, preserving 66, shortcake 67, stewed 66, 90
apples, filled with liver and bacon 78
arthritis pain 107
Austrian drink 67

B

baby bathing 105
bacon 67
baking cakes, common problems when 72
baking in bulk 103
ballpoint ink stains 8
ballpoint pens, dried out 95
banana cake 67, waffles 67, in stuffing 67, ripening 67, prevent browning 68
barrier cream 105
bath cleaning 29
bath plug tips 28
bath towels, washing 32, as mats 32
bathroom cleaning tips 28 — 33
bathroom mirror 28
bean sprouts 68
beaten egg whites 75
bedspreads, ironing 40
beef casserole from cheap cut 105
beetroot fried 68, raw 68, pickled 68
belts, storing 97
berry and red fruit on white cotton stains 8
bib substitute 106
birds, keeping away 56, 58, 59
biscuits, crisp 68
black boot marks on rubber tiles 44
black clothes, washing 34
blackberry jam as topping 68
blackcurrant jam as accompaniment 68
blankets fragrance 34
blood stains 8
blu-tack 94
boiled eggs 74
boiling water, saving 102
bone-handled knives, cleaning 49
boots, waterproofing 36
bottle smell, removing 99
bottling fruit 76
brandy snaps 80

brass cleaning 52 — 53
bread bin, musty 25
bread dough rising 77
bread pudding, savoury 88
breadcrumbs 69
breadcrumbs add bulk 103
breakfast cereal substitute 92
briquettes for fire 101
broad beans 93
broccoli as sandwich filling 87
brown sugar 89
budget living 101
bulb storage 54
bulk buy cheese 103
bulk soap 31
burglar-proofing 94
burn marks on plates 20
burning without incinerator 61
burnt toast 69
burnt-on food 16
butter softening 89

C

cabbage, chopping cooked 71
cabbage, freshen 92
cake filling 75
cake tin hot from oven 70
cake tins, rusty 16
cake-baking, common problems in 72
cakes, keeping fresh 70
calico, unbleached 41
cameo, cleaning 52
can openers 23
candles 95, 101
candlewick bedcover, drying 39

cappuccino machine, cleaning 26
car oil for painting stakes 65
car oil on concrete 62
car tyre walls, cleaning 65
care labels 38
carpet indent marks 97
carrot juice in gravy 69
carrot tops 71
carrots, freshen 93
casseroles, budget cooking of 101
casseroles, thicken 91
catching drips when washing walls 62
cats, keeping away 57
cauliflower, freshen 92
celery, freshen 92, 93
cement on clothing 34
cereal substitute 92
chalks, protecting 107
chamois leather, cleaning 48
cheap beef cut casserole 105
cheap carpet, upholstery deodorant 101
cheap fruit yoghurt 104
cheese sauce 70, waffles 70, and mushrooms 70
chewing gum stains 8
chicken soup 71
chicken, crispy 73
chiffon scarf care 34
child's bedroom decorating 105
child's plaster cast 105
children rolling out of bed, preventing 106
children's party invites 105
children's play area 106
children's sandals 106

children, amusing in kitchen 105
children, hints for 105
china cabinet care 44
chips in bath 62, on refrigerator 62, in white wood 62
chocolate icing for lamingtons 71
chocolate stains 8
chocolate, melted 78
chopping board, non-slip 20
chopping board, onion, garlic smells on 27
chopping cooked cabbage , silverbeet 71
Christmas cake icing, soften 71
Christmas planning 105
Christmas tree care 55
chrome surfaces, cleaning 45
chrysanthemums, wind-blown 61
cinnamon 71
cleaning hints 44 — 53
clingfilm, melted 17
coconut cake 70
coffee figs 72
coffee stains 8
coffee with orange, lemon flavour 72
cold water washing 103
colds 108
coleslaw 72
concrete steps made non-slip 64
concrete, moss and mould on 63, oil on 62, paint on 63
continental-style mustard 73
cooking smells 25
copper cleaning 51 — 52, 53

copper saucepans 17
cordial 73
cork floors, cleaning 48
cork, replacing 99
corned beef 80, tender 91
correspondence 96
cough or sore throat relief 108
cracked heels 109
cramp in legs and feet 108
crayon stains on blackboard 12, on lino 12, on vinyl wallpaper 13
crayons, protecting 107
creaking floor boards 65
cream stains on grey sweatshirt 11
creaming brown sugar 89
creases in lace netting 40
crispy chicken 73
crispy pork crackling 85
crumble mixture 73
crumbly cheese 73
crystal vase, chipped 95
crystallise flowers 62
cucumber 73
cupboards, musty 25, 47
cups, discoloured 20
curly leaf on peach trees 55
curry stains 13
curry, overspiced 81
curtains framing windows 63
custard 73
cut flowers 55, 56
cut-glass vases, cleaning 47
cutlery, washing 20
cuttings, collection of 56

D

dampening hair 111

dandruff treatment with salt 111
dark clothes, washing 34, fluff on 112
darken mahogany cabinet 62
decorate iced cake 69
defrosting, cold hands when 22
diamond rings 51, 52
dirty dishes 103
dishcloths, grubby 25
dishwasher odours 20
do-it-yourself tips 61 — 65
document storage in freezer 100
dough crust 69
draught sealers 102
drawer, tight-fitting 100
drying clothes 38 — 40
duck, basting 67
dustless duster 46

E

earrings, avoid damage to 108
economical all-purpose cleaner 101, 103
egg beaters, cleaning 21
egg sandwich filling 75
egg substitute for pie crusts 103
egg substitute, evaporated milk as 74
eggs 74 — 75
electric iron, cleaning 40
emerald, cleaning 52
enamel bath cleaning 29
evaporated milk 74
eye pencils 110

F

fat, remove from soups and stews 86
feather duvet care 35
feet, tired 111
felt pen stains on plastic 13
filling for cake 75
fingermarks on polished furniture 45
fingermarks stains on walls 13
firelighters 102
fish fillets in ale 76, cakes 76, steaming 76, stock 76
fish slime stains 9
fish smells on velvet 42
flavouring tricks 74
flies, keeping away 96, repellent 96, specks 96
flies, repelling with herbs 25
floor boards, creaking 65
floor polish recipes 46
floral display in winter 55
flour 76
flour and grain storage 91
flower arrangement 59
flower water, stop smells in 50
fluff on dark clothing 43
fly specks on mirrors, windows 46
foil as scouring pad 26
foil in vases 55
foil, uses for 92
food tips 66 — 93
formica bench, scratched 20
fragrant linen cupboard 96
freezer labels 22
freezer smells 26

freezer, defrosting 21
freezing soups and stews 21
fridge smells 26
fridge, cleaning 21, defrosting 21, odours 22, mildew 22, seals 21
fried eggs 74
fruit bottling 76, stewing 76
fruit ripening 87
fruit stains on table linen 13
fruit stains on white woollens 9
fruit-flavoured icing 75
frying pan, to season 16, cleaning 16, 17
fumes in kitchen 26
funnel, eggshell, foil as 23
furniture polish 45
fuse wire 96

G

garden hose 56
garden stakes painted with oil 65
garden tap 55
garden-soiled hands, cleaning 56
gardening gloves 56
gardening tips 54 — 61
gardening trousers, padded 58
garlic breath, countering 109
garlic companion planting 56
garlic, onion smells on hands 27, on chopping board 27
garlic, storing 76
general hints 94 — 113
ginger beer corks 96
ginger storage 76
gingerbread, leftover 77

glass in picture frames, cleaning 48
glass, prevent from cracking 99
glasses, keep paint off 64
glasses, scratches on 99
glasses, washing 21
glaze for fruit pies 76
gloves, washing 35
gold jewellery 51, 52
gooseberries 57
grained bread 92
grapefruit 77
grass stains on white cotton 9
grater, cleaning 20
grater, getting peel from 72
grater, run cold water over 87
grating orange, lemon rinds 81
gravy 76
grease on stove 18, on bench 20
grease on suede shoes 9
grease spots on carpet 14
greased baking tins 77
greaseproof paper 77
greasy collars and cuffs 9
greasy marks on upholstered chair backs 14
greenfly 56
grouting, cleaning 33

H

hair brush and comb soak 111
hair brushing 109
hair conditioner, home-made 109
hand cream 107
hand measure 97

hands, cleaning, softening after gardening 110
hands, onion, garlic smells on 27
hanging baskets, watering 61
hardened paint brushes, to soften 64
hats, storage of 97
heat marks on polished wood 14
heavy trunks stored 100
herbal bath 109
hiccups cure 109
honey in rhubarb 86
honey substitute for sugar 77
horseradish sauce substitute 91
hot water thermostat 101
hot-water bottle 94
hub caps 63
hydrangeas, wool scourers used for 54

I

iced cake decoration 69
indent marks on carpet 97
ink stains on leather 15
ink stains on linen 10, on white blouses and shirts 10
ink stains on plastic 13
iron, cleaning electric 40
ironing clothes 40 — 41
ironing shortcuts 40
itchy insect bits 109
itchy woollen jumper 43
ivory piano keys, yellowing 51
ivory, cleaning 52

J

jade, cleaning, 52
jam-sweetened tea 77
jammed locks 97
jar storage 98
jelly and ice cream dessert 74
jelly for children 82
jelly in minutes 77
jerseys, drying 39
jet, cleaning 52
jewellery care 51, 52

K

kerosene as fly repellent 47
kettle element, furred 23
kitchen cleaning tips 16 — 27
kneehighs, uses for 97
knitwear washing 37
knots in gold chain, untangling 100

L

laminated benchtop stains 15
laminated tabletop stains 15
lamington chocolate icing 71
laundry bag, travelling 43
laundry tips 34 — 43
lawn fertiliser 61
leaf curl in stone fruit trees 59
leather furniture, refresh 49
leather jacket collar 43
leftover lamb 104
leftover paint 63
leftovers, storage in fridge 22
lemon and honey drink 77
lemon flavour coffee 72
lemon juice economy 104
lemons, storage 91
lemons, uses for 84 — 85

lettuce 57, 78
lettuce leaves for soup 104
lettuce, freshen 93
lids, opening jar, bottle 23
light bulbs wiped with perfume 101
light saving 102, 103
limp vegetables, freshen 92
linen cupboard, fragrant 96
lino lifting 63, laying 63
lino, cleaning 49
lipstick stains 10
liquid soap recipes 32, 35
locks, jammed 97
looking after yourself 107 — 113
low-fat toasted sandwiches 78
luggage labels, run-proofing 97
lumpy ingredients 78

M

macadamia nuts, opening 81
mahogany cabinet, darkening 62
maidenhair fern care 57
mail tip 95
marble, cleaning 45
marrow 78
marshmallows, add to custard 73
mascara remains 110
mashed potatoes, watery 78
meat loaf 89
meat patties, freezing 92
meringue 79
metal earrings, avoid damage to 108

microwave cleaning 19, freshness 19
mildew on bath mats 32, on grouting 32
mildew on shower curtain 30
mildew on thermal drapes 47
milk boiling 79, boiling over 79
Milo in fridge 79
mince additions 79
mince goes further 104
mince, freezing 79
mint jelly 90
mint sauce 79
mint with potatoes 79
mirror cleaning 28, 50
mirrors, stop misting 28, clean bathroom 28
mixing bowl 84
mohair rugs 98
moisture in cupboards 25
moss and mould on concrete 63
mothballs 99
mousse for children, party 80
mouth ulcers 108
mud stains 10
mushrooms 74, 80
mustard, continental-style 73
musty bread bin 25, cupboards 25, 47

N

nail polish 110, 111
nail polish bottles 110
nail varnish stains on rayons 10
nails, hammering 61
nappies, bleaching 105

nappy care 36, stains 36
nashi pears, ripening 87
needle or pin lost 100
net curtain repair 97
new overalls 36
new sheets 36
newspaper in wet shoes 99
non-pouring tomato sauce 92
non-slip concrete steps 64
nuts and fruit for cakes 93
nuts, cracking 80
nuts for cakes 80

O

oil on concrete 62
oil stains on imitation suede 11
oily hair 110
old socks, uses for 98
olive oil stains 11
omelette pan 17
onion, garlic smells on hands, 27, on chopping board 27
onions, boiling 80, without tears 80, peeling 80, roasting 80,
onions, storage 58
opals, cleaning 52
opening bottle, jar lids 23
orange flavour coffee 72
orange freezing 81, garnish 81, cake 81
ornaments 99
oven cleaning 19, smells 19
oven switches, faded 17
overalls, new 36, dirty 37
overspiced curry 81
overspiced stew 81

P

packing cases stored 100
paint brushes, soften 64
paint spots on concrete 63
paint stains 11
paint tray, lining 63
painted woodwork, cleaning 47, 48
painting for children 106
painting window frames 64
paintwork, cleaning 44
pancakes 66
pantihose ladder 111
pantihose, protecting 110
pantihose, uses for 97
paper towel, uses for 25
parquet floors, cleaning 48
parsley dried 81, freezing 81, quick-dried 82
parsnip seeds 58
parsnips and carrots cooked 82
party ice 22
partying on wet night 98
pasta 82
pastry glaze 91
pastry tips 82
patty tins, blackened 16
pavlova 82
peanut butter 83
peanut butter in child's hair 106
peanuts, toasting 88
pearls, cleaning 52
peeler, vegetable 24
pepper pot 83
perspiration stains 11
phone call savings 95
piano keys, yellowing ivory 51

pickled onion jar smells 26
picnic tablecloths 98
picture glass, cleaning 48
picture hooks 100
pie, reheating 83, heating frozen 83, baking 83
pigskin shoes, softening 41
pikelets 83
pikelets, savoury 88
pineapple cider 84
pineapple juice, uses for fresh 83
piping bag 84
plant care during holiday 54
plant protector 54
plaster, removing from skin 111
plastic bag drying 95
plastic bread bags as shoe covers 64
plastic picnic knives 58
plates, burn marks on 20
plug, protecting 35
poached eggs 74
polished floors, cleaning 48
polished furniture, cleaning 48
pork chop coating 84
pork crackling 84
pork, roast loin of 87
pot lid storage 17
pot plants, outdoors 58
potato suggestions 85, freezing 85
pots and pans, cleaning 16 - 17
potting tip 58
poultry, stuffing 86
preschooler and colours 106
preserving flowers by waxing 59
protecting bus passes 106
prune pulp 86
pumpkin storage 90
pumpkins 59

Q
quick dessert 86

R
rambling rose support 54
recipes, store 91
recycle can labels 102
recycle refill packs 86
recycling food 24, plastic bottles 24
red fruit on white cotton stains 8
red wine spills on carpet 14, on table linen 14
refill packs, recycle 86
refrigerator; see fridge, freezer
repotting small plants 59
rhubarb leaves prevent rust 59
rhubarb with honey 86, with jelly 86
rhubarb, tartness 91
rice, steamed 86, non-stick 87, in salt shaker 87
ring stuck on finger 101
ripen fruit 87
roast vegetable power saving 104
rolled icing 69
room heating tips 102, 103
root ginger storage 76

rubber gloves, dust inside 96
rubbish bag 64, 98
rubbish bin liners 26
ruby, cleaning 52
rust stains on metal 15
rust stains on white shirt collar 11

S

salt and pepper 88
salt as dandruff treatment 111
salty taste 68
sandpit 106
sapphire, cleaning 52
saucepan knobs from corks 102
saucepans as scoop 92
saucepans, cleaning 16 - 17, 24
sausage casserole savings 104
sausage rolls 66
sausages 88
saute 88
savoury bread pudding 88
savoury pikelets 88
scar tissue 110
scarves, storing 100
scented sachet, home-made 109
scones, freshen up 88, keep fresh 89
scorch marks 12
scorch marks on cotton or linen 40
scouring pads, rust-free 18
scrambled eggs 74
scratches on glasses 99
seeds in bulk 54
seeds, planting 55, 58, 60

separate egg yolk and white 75
shagpile carpet 99
shaving cream as upholstery cleaner 103
sheepskin rug, washing 37
sheets, drying on line 39
shine on trousers 37
shoe cleaning 41 — 42
shoe covers, plastic bread bags as 64
shoe laces for children 105
shoe polish, softening 41
shoes, black marks 41
shortbread slices 88
shortcake filling 89
shower curtain cleaning 30, 31
shower door cleaning 30
silk colours, setting 37
silk flowers, dusting 45
silk scarves 99
silver cleaner 53
silverbeet 88
silverbeet, chopping cooked 71
silverbeet, freshen 92
sink, blocked 18, cleaning 18
skirts on coat hanger 99
slugs 60
small cakes, storage 90
smell of cat urine in shoes 42
smell of diesel fumes in clothing 42
smells 25, 26, 27, 42, 43
smells in fridge-freezer 26
smells in pickled onion jar 26
smelly shoes 42
snails 60

soap scum on glass and tiles 31
sock, use for cleaning 48
socks, keeping pairs together 37
socks, uses for old 98
soft cake filling 75
soot on carpets 44
sour cream leftover 89
souvenir teatowels 99
spatulas, loose 23
spectacles, cleaning 108
spiced fruits 89 — 90
spillovers on stove 17
spray-cleaning bottle, uses for empty 45
spring onions 90
squeaky door hinges 100
stain removal 8 — 15
    ballpoint ink 8
    berry and red fruit on white cotton 8
    blood 8
    chewing gum 8
    chocolate 8
    coffee 8
    crayon on blackboard 12, lino 12, vinyl wallpaper 13
    cream on grey sweatshirt 11
    curry 13
    felt pen on plastic 13
    fingermarks on walls 13
    fish slime 9
    fruit on white woollens 9
    fruit stains on table linen 13
    grass on white cotton 9
    grease on suede shoes 9
    grease spots on carpet 14
    greasy collars and cuffs 9
    greasy marks on upholstered chair backs 14
    heat marks on polished wood 14
    ink on leather 15
    ink on linen 10, on white blouses and shirts 10
    ink on plastic 13
    lipstick 10
    laminated benchtop stains 15
    laminated tabletop stains 15
    mud 10
    nail varnish on rayons 10
    oil on imitation suede 11
    olive oil 11
    paint 11
    perspiration 11
    red fruit on white cotton 8
    red wine spills on carpet 14, on table linen 14
    rust on metal 15
    rust on white shirt collar 11
    scorch marks 12
    sticky labels on polyester 12
    water stains on glass vases 15, on mattress 15
    white correction fluid 10
    yellow fruit juice on grey sweatshirt 11
    yellowish vinyl on bedhead 15
stained hands 77
stained teaspoons 21

stainless steel, high gloss 46
stains, general hints 7
starched garment care 36
static in carpets 44
static shock from car, preventing 100
steam iron, filling 40
steamed vegetables, avoid scalding with 87
stewed apples 90
stewing fruit 76
stews, budget cooking of 101
stews, thicken 91
stickers on windscreen, remove 64
sticky labels on containers 26
sticky labels on furniture 49, on glass 50
sticky labels on polyester 12
stiff bathroom cabinet doors 32
stovetop elements 102
strawberries 90
stray cat 100
stuffing poultry 86
stuffing, leftover 90
sty on eyelid 111
styrofoam packing sheets 100
sulphur deposits on windows 50
sunburn relief 111
sunflowers, planting 58
sweater, stop stretching 37, washing 38
sweet pasty glaze 91
swinging cupboard door 94
syrup, prevent crystallising 68

T

T-shirts, drying 39
tablecloths as teatowels 101
tamarillos, stewed 90
tanning smell in suede jacket 42
tar on hands 110
tea sweetened with jam 77
tea, coffee for large groups 70
teabag catering size 95
teabag, uses for 21
tears from onions, preventing 80
teaspoons, stained 21
telephone books for reference 98
tenderise meat 91
thermal drapes, mildew on 47, separating 50
thermal sulphur deposits on windows 50
thicken stews, casseroles 91, vegetable soups 92, mashed potatoes 78
thinning out plants 60
tidying the house 101
tight-fitting drawers 100
time out 111
tin openers 23
tired feet 111
toast rack as letter holder 61
toast, burnt 69
toasted sandwiches, low-fat 78
toilet bowl washing 31
toilet cleaners 31, odours 31, rolls 31
tomato plant stakes 60
tomato sauce not pouring 92

tomato, stop soggy 70
tomatoes, freezing 92, peeling 92
tomatoes, stop squashing 70
toothache relief 111
toothpaste holder 32, remnants in tube 33
towel care 35
towel in car 96
toy storage 106, 107
toys with sewn on clothes, washing 38
turquoise, cleaning 52
tying up plants 61

U

umbrella 99
unbleached calico 41
urine smell on mattress 49

V

vacuum flask, cleaning 26
vases, stop smell of water in 50
vegetable soup, thicken 92
vegetables, gathering 61
velvet curtains, flattened pile 46
venetian blinds, cleaning 46, 48
vinegar, uses for 48

W

waffle iron heat test 91
waffles 66
wallpaper, remove 64
walnuts, store shelled 93
warm oven economy 104
warming room 102
warts 112
washing machine smells 34
washing powder storage 38
waste disposal 18
water stains on glass vases 15, on mattress 15
watering indoor pot plants 60, on holiday 60
watering plants 54
waterproof fabrics 37
waterproof leaking vase 100
waterproofing boots 36
watery mashed potatoes 78
weeds 60
whipped cream 73
white correction fluid stains 10
white icing 70
white leather shoes, covering 42
white sauce, quick and easy 86
window cleaner 49
window frames, painting 64
windows, cleaning 49, 50
windscreen stickers, remove 64
wooden hairbrushes 51
wooden spoons and utensils 23
wooden swing, protecting 107
woodwork, cleaning 47
wool underlays, substitute for 98
woollen jumper, itchy 43
woollens, revitalising 37
worn children's blankets, renewing 103

wrapping presents 94
wrought-iron furniture 65

Y

yellow fruit juice stains on
    grey sweatshirt 11
yellowish stains on vinyl
    bedhead 15
yolks, leftover 75
Yorkshire pudding 93

Z

zip, metal 96, plastic 96
zips in wash 34

YOUR NOTES

YOUR NOTES